The Moral Tradition in English Fiction, 1785-1850

The University Press of New England

Sponsoring Institutions
Brandeis University
Clark University
Dartmouth College
University of New Hampshire
University of Rhode Island
University of Vermont

The Moral Tradition in English Fiction, 1785-1850

by Samuel Pickering, Jr.

Published for Dartmouth College by
The University Press of New England
Hanover, New Hampshire
1976

Preface

In 1819 Andrew Reed published *No Fiction*. Despite its subtitle, "A Narrative Founded on Recent and Interesting Facts," *No Fiction* was a novel. The story of two young school teachers, James Douglas and Charles Lefevre, the book illustrated the dangers of reading fiction. When "Duty called Mr. Douglas" from London, Lefevre became the companion of Wallis, who had the revealing habit of coiling his body around chairs. Wallis introduced Lefevre to his sister, an inveterate reader of "moral tales." Led astray by this daughter of Eve, Lefevre became "a most determined and indefatigable novel reader." From these "indecent rhapsodies," it was but a short moral step down to strong drink, gambling, and the theater, which itself "opened an easy passage to the brothel." As his sins accumulated, Lefevre suffered Adamite pangs of conscience. Unable to drown his sorrows "in oblivion," he considered suicide. Finally, in desperation he enlisted as a soldier. On board ship sailing for Canada, a fellow soldier gave him a Bible. Making it his "companion all day" and his "pillow all night," he fed upon this "angels' food" until "pure, spiritual, living, and life-imparting" knowledge flowed into his soul. In the wilds of the New World, Lefevre became the Christian Hero, "benevolently endeavouring to benefit others." When he returned to

England, Douglas welcomed him, and together they defended the true faith against Wallis and the novel.

Reed debated for a long time before publishing *No Fiction*. On completing the manuscript, he wrote agonizingly, "What to do with it, I know not. I must let others judge for me. If it is thought unlikely to do good, it will never enter the press; for, after all my pains, it will be worthless in my esteem. Source of Wisdom, do Thou direct me! Thou has put it in my heart to perform this work. It has been executed with *many, many* prayers; and Thou canst give it a Divine Blessing!" Speaking through his friends, the "Source of Wisdom" urged Reed to publish. Before doing so, Reed dedicated the manuscript to his "Gracious Saviour." "Let it be a guide to the ignorant," he prayed humbly, "a beacon to the careless, and a stay to the unstable."

Reed's prayers were answered. *No Fiction* became a best seller, running through five editions in two years, being translated into French and Dutch and enjoying a "large sale" in the United States. A literary reputation, however, is not a joy forever: Andrew Reed and *No Fiction* are now forgotten. Reed's dilemma, his religiosity, and the novel's quixotic attack on fiction strike the modern reader as at best quaint and at worst ridiculous.

Tides of taste and scholarship ebb and flow. In today's popular schools of criticism, which delight in imposing twentieth-century sensibilities upon nineteenth-century writers, there exists little opportunity to breathe critical life back into Reed's dry bones. This book may not entirely escape the taint of subjectivity, but my approach is *in flagrante delicto* historical. Readers who believe that critical truth is psychological, affective, or phenomenological had better turn back now, for my concern is to show that the great tradition of the early nineteenth-century English novel is the moral tradition. Instead of bleaching in a cultural wasteland, the works of Andrew Reed, John Cunningham, Legh Richmond, and Hannah More lie in the mainstream of the moral English novel.

Through discussions of the growth and influence of the Sunday School movement and the readers it produced, I intend to show that evangelical standards became the primary critical yardstick by which English Christian readers measured literature. As the novel fell from critical grace during the early years of the Napoleonic Wars, the seeds of its regeneration were planted by the writers of religious tracts, in particular by the Clapham Sect and the *Cheap Repository Tracts*. Crucial to the novel's regaining the respect it had enjoyed during the middle of the eighteenth century was the success of Hannah More's "dramatic sermon," *Coelebs in Search of a Wife*. From *Coelebs* it was a long literary but short thematic hop to Walter Scott and a skip and a jump to Charles Dickens. By examining three of Dickens' novels as case studies, I illustrate the rise-and-fall pattern of the moral tradition in the Victorian novel.

Pursuing the moral tradition, I have become something of a critical Polyphemus, oftentimes ignoring the men among the sheep. For example, I have paid little attention to the economic reasons for the novel's success. Furthermore, I have focused on but few writers and have said little or nothing about Jane Austen, Charlotte Brontë, or George Eliot. In defense let me say I think my "religious" approach could and should be applied to these authors, but my scope is modest, and I thought it more valuable to see deep rather than broad. As a result I have concentrated on Dickens.

No critic has a self-pollenizing mind. Like a Jamesian artist, the critic converts air-blown grains of suggestion into manuscripts. For my part, I am indebted to many scholars whom I have met only through their writings, specifically Richard D. Altick, Ford K. Brown, R. S. Crane, Robert Mayo, Kathleen Tillotson, and J. M. S. Tompkins. Likewise, I have spent many happy hours in libraries amid piles of musty books. At Princeton University, Princeton Seminary, Dartmouth College, Vanderbilt University, the British Museum, University College London, and Dr. Williams's Library, librarians have loomed before me as a pillar of fire by night when I stumbled lost in the dark wilderness of evangelicalism. Lastly, I will always be indebted to the English Department of Princeton University for laying the foundation of my approach. In particular, my heart still leaps up appreciatively when I remember the time Mr. Carlos Baker spent with me as teacher and friend.

Hanover, New Hampshire   S.P.
August 1975

Contents

The Moral Tradition in English Fiction, 1785-1850

Introduction

In the late seventeenth and early eighteenth centuries, latitudinarians became a powerful force in the Established Church. Reacting against doctrinaire Puritanism, broad church divines such as Isaac Barrow, John Scott, Samuel Clarke, and John Tillotson attempted to turn Anglicanism into a moral system emphasizing charity instead of Christ and goodness instead of grace. Relegating doctrine to the background and substituting good deeds in its place, Clarke wrote that "zeal for particular forms and ceremonies, more than for Virtue and Religion itself" hindered "the growth of Christian Charity, and, like the Worm at the Root of *Jonah's* Gourd" ate out "the vitals of true Religion." Tillotson agreed, telling his congregation that it was better to be useful to others than to quarrel about doubtful and uncertain doctrines. "To be of a kind and obliging disposition, of a tender and compassionate spirit, sensible of the straits and miseries of others, so as to be ready to ease and relieve them," he wrote, was "the happiest spirit and temper in the world."[1]

In opposition to Calvinistic emphasis on the depravity of man, which they thought fragmented the Christian commu-

1. Samuel Clarke, *Works* (London, 1738), I, 299. Thos. Birch, ed., *The Works of John Tillotson* (London, 1820), II, 203; IX, 83.

3

nity and impeded good deeds, latitudinarians stressed the importance of benevolent feelings. For Barrow the idea that men were naturally enemies was a monstrous paradox going not only against common sense but also the intention of "the Author of our nature." Moreover the true Christian contracted society with others so that he, in Scott's words, could "be ready to every good Work, and like Fields of Spices" scatter his "Perfumes through all the Neighbourhood." For Scott, society was absolutely necessary to cherish and preserve in us our natural benevolence towards one another." Out of society, man's nature degenerated and "instead of being inclined to assist" grew "always most salvage and barbarous to his own kind." The spontaneous overflow of powerful feeling, brought about by a sympathetic identification with others and leading to good deeds, became the hallmark of the Christian. "The frame of our nature so far disposeth us thereto," Barrow wrote, "that our bowels are touched with sensible pain upon the view of any calamitous object; our fancy is disturbed at the report of any disaster befalling any person; we can hardly see or read a Tragedy without motions of compassion."[2]

Spreading beyond the church, latitudinarian theology influenced almost all areas of English thought. In literature the cult of sensibility and the man of feeling were direct offshoots from Barrow's "motions of compassion." Mirroring broad church concerns, criticism demanded that the novel be a par-

2. John Tillotson, ed., *The Works of the Learned Isaac Barrow* (London, 1683), I, 350, 374. John Scott, *The Christian Life from Its Beginning to its Consummation in Glory* (London, 1681), pp. 176–177, 185.

able teaching Christian charity. In her *Progress of Romance,* Clara Reeve preached a latitudinarian sermon on the moral effects of literature, writing of the novel: "Such books cannot be too strongly recommended, as under the disguise of fiction, warm the heart with the love of virtue, and by that means, excite the reader to the practice of it." When confronted with novels which toed the correct moral line by moving readers first "to shed the sacred drops of sympathy" and then to benevolent acts, criticism, wrote the *Critical Review,* "smooths his brow, and takes off his spectacles, willing to see no fault."[3]

Like tracing the evolution of man, pinpointing the origins of the moral novel is chancy. New and embarrassing ancestors will forever turn up in the backwaters of Elizabethan pamphlets. Nevertheless, with apologies to all who see deeper into the past of things, I want to begin with Samuel Richardson. For Anna Barbauld, as for most eighteenth and early nineteenth-century critics, Richardson was "the father of the modern novel of the serious or pathetic kind." Evoking "motions of compassion," *Pamela* preached the rewards of virtue and the virtue of charity. The enthusiastic reception of the novel by Richardson's friend Aaron Hill was almost typical. "It will live on, thro' posterity," Hill wrote, "with such unbounded extent of good consequences, that twenty ages to come may be the better and wiser, for its influence." "Who could have dreamt," Hill exclaimed, that "he should find under the modest disguise of a *novel,* all the *soul* of reli-

3. Clara Reeve, *The Progress of Romance* (London, 1785), p. 126. *Critical Review,* 63 (1787), 77.

gion, good-breeding, discretion, good-nature, wit, fancy, fine thought, and morality?"[4]

Although Fielding was certainly not among them, most readers approved Richardson's latitudinarianism and seconded Hill's judgment. Within a few years, the novel of sensibility had become a prominent feature of the country's literary landscape; and Richardson was known almost mythically as "the English moralist" whose works constituted "the best and most applicable system of morality, for young people, that ever appeared in any language." Suffering through hurricanes of distress, scores of heroes and heroines provided the "feeling bosom" with "numberless opportunities of indulging the luxury of tears." After the phenomenal success of Henry Mackenzie's *The Man of Feeling* (1771), the novel of sensibility appeared to have achieved permanent respectability.[5]

In this case, however, popular appearances were deceiving. Although the afflatus of charitable sensibility had greatly muted criticism, an undercurrent of ethical poetics had run against the celebration of the novel since the beginning of the century. Traditional moralists argued that novels and romances undermined reason by appealing to the imagination, thereby freeing man from the restraints of conscience. In *The Universal Spectator, and Weekly Journal,* a writer declared in 1730 that romances ruined "more Virgins than *Masquerades* or *Brothels.*" "I leave you to judge," the writer warned, "what an excellent Housewife a Damsel is likely to make, who

4. Anna Barbauld, ed., *The Correspondence of Samuel Richardson* (London, 1804), I, xi. Aaron Hill, *Works* (London, 1753), II, 286, 290.
5. *Critical Review,* 12 (1762), 204. *Monthly Review,* 24 (1761), 260. *London Magazine,* 38 (1769), 438–439.

had read the *Persian Tales*, 'till she fancies herself a *Sultana*."
Behind the writer's immediate focus on women's plackets lay
the belief that novels corrupted the mind by appealing to the
imagination. According to Dr. Johnson, "Works of Fiction"
were particularly dangerous "to the Young, the Ignorant,
and the Idle, to whom they serve as Lectures of Conduct,
and Introductions into Life." Since the minds of such persons were "unfurnished with Ideas," "not fixed by Principle," and "not formed by Experience," they were "easily
susceptible of Impressions" and "following the Current of
Fancy" open "to every false Suggestion and partial Account."
Because of this, Johnson stressed, a novelist had to be careful that his "Lectures" always taught that virtue was "the
highest Proof of a superior Understanding, and the only
solid Basis of Greatness" while vice was "the natural Consequence of narrow Thoughts" and ended in "Ignominy."[6]

Because Richardson's success focused attention on the
novel, journals such as the *London Magazine*, the *Critical
Review*, and the *Monthly Review* developed rudimentary
ethical and literary standards of criticism. Critical subtlety
was unnecessary, since most novels were ground out by hacks
following the trail of tears left by *Pamela* and *Clarissa*. Of
such a tear-jerker, *The Unhappy Wife*, the *London Magazine* wrote, "We will not add distress to an unhappy wife by
saying directly what we think of her work. We shall therefore add that the lady now under consideration, has made
us very unhappy." When, however, a journal discovered an

6. "A Letter to a Lady Concerning Books of Piety and Romances,"
The Universal Spectator, and Weekly Journal, 91 (4 July 1730). Samuel
Johnson, *The Rambler*, 4 (31 March 1750), 19–21, 24.

improper novel, wit was forgotten and the ethical yardstick rapped down. Reviewing *Lycoris: or, the Greek Courtezan*, the *Critical Review* stated tersely, "this is one of those novels which tends to imbrute the human species, and adds spurs to the illicit correspondence between the sexes."[7]

With the spread of circulating libraries filled with the "overflowings of dissipated brains" in the 1770's and 1780's, journals became less tolerant of hackneyed tales of sensibility. Of *The Sorrows of the Heart*, the *Monthly Review* wrote wearily, "the modern novel affords us nothing like variety. 'Soup for breakfast, soup for dinner, and soup for supper,' as the libertine in the comedy observes of his wife." For the *Critical Review*, it was a simple matter in 1785 to sketch the plot of a typical novel. "A hero and a heroine," the journal declared, "each endowed with every perfection, must see each other by chance, and become instantly enamoured. They must labour through two or three volumes; and, if no churlish father, or ambitious aunt, is in the way, they must have a reasonable quantity of doubt and suspicion, infused by false friends. The lady too, may be forced away by a disappointed lover, and rescued miraculously. At last, one or other must be near death, either by accident or premeditated violence, and may recover or not, according to the disposition of the author. This is the skeleton of a modern novel: sentiments, character, or language, are of little consequence."[8]

These statements by the leading monthly reviews not only show exasperation with predictable plots but also imply a

7. *London Magazine*, 39 (1770), 378. *Critical Review*, 11 (1761), 338.
8. *Monthly Review*, 76 (1787), 531. *Critical Review*, 59 (1785), 316; 62 (1786), 149.

growing distrust of sensibility. As the eighteenth century unfolded and the novel of sensibility became phenomenally
popular, critical sophistication grew. Although sensibility was
still generally respected, by the 1780's journals were calling
Fancy "a runaway tit," standing "in particular need of the
curb." No longer were good deeds thought the necessary consequence of tears. Essayists in the Johnsonian tradition
warned readers against possible harmful effects of sensibility.
Most alarming was the dissociation of sensibility and practical charity. "Nothing is more dangerous," Anna Barbauld
wrote, "than to let virtuous impressions of any kind pass
through the mind without producing their proper effect. The
awakenings of remorse, virtuous shame and indignation, the
glow of moral approbation, if they do not lead to action, grow
less and less vivid every time they recur, till at length the
mind grows absolutely callous." By 1785 even Henry Mackenzie had had serious thoughts about the abuses of sensibility. "In the enthusiasm of sentiment," he wrote, "there is
much the same danger as in the enthusiasm of religion, of
substituting certain impulses and feelings of what may be
called a visionary kind, in the place of real practical duties,
which in morals, as in theology, we might not improperly
denominate *good works*."⁹

Contributing to sensibility's loss of critical favor were factors other than the fear that good deeds and "motions of
compassion" were not intimately related. Some critics thought
the novel itself was suffering through moral and literary dog

9. *Monthly Review*, 75 (1786), 468. J. and A. L. Aikin, *Miscellaneous
Pieces* (London, 1773), pp. 211–212. Henry Mackenzie, *The Lounger*, 20
(18 June 1785), 79.

days. At Oxford Thomas Munro attributed what he thought was a decline in the novel's quality to sentimentalists who wrote "rhapsodies of nonsense" instead of copying Richardson's "delicate and refined sentiment." To some extent the spread of literacy contributed to sensibility's decline. What was good for the pampered lady of the manor was not necessarily good for the chambermaid dusting in the hall. By giving mechanicals inflated imaginative views of themselves, sensibility indirectly threatened the hierarchical structure of society. According to Munro the characters of "sentimental novels," sentimental Abigails, gallant footmen, and rhetorical shoemakers, did "a material injury to that part of the nation, who, when they have shut up shop, wet their thumbs and spell through a novel."[10] More important to the decline of sensibility, however, was the changing religious climate. In form, if not in name, evangelicalism was slowly replacing latitudinarianism as the most significant religious movement of the century. Stressing objective doctrine, evangelicalism philosophically clashed with sensibility, whose subjective appeal tended toward a secular ethics outside the restraints of religious dogma. In conjunction with the general conservative reaction to the French Revolution, this theological shift had great significance for the reading public and the novel. Modifying the novel and critical poetics for their didactic purposes, religious educators and apologists in the last years of the eighteenth and first years of the nineteenth centuries determined not only the expectations of the reading public, which they had educated in Sunday Schools, but also the form and content of the early Victorian novel.

10. Thomas Munro, *Olla Podrida*, 15 (23 June 1787), 86–88.

Chapter 1
The Sunday School Movement
New Readers and the Novel

In his *History of the English People,* the nineteenth century historian John Richard Green stated that "the Sunday Schools established by Mr. Raikes of Gloucester" were "the beginnings of popular education." At the start of the twentieth century the Sunday School enthusiast John James Wright wrote colorfully: "As Homer is called the Father of Poetry, and Herodotus the Father of History, so Robert Raikes may be looked upon as the Founder of the Sunday School System." To us Wright's comparisons seem ludicrous. Herodotus and Homer, part of the glory that was Greece, are familiar to every schoolboy. In contrast historians have been largely indifferent to the Sunday School movement, preferring instead to write political history or traditional studies of great men. Nicknamed "Bobby Wild Goose" because of his inexhaustible energy, Robert Raikes certainly did not have the stature of a great man. But his "botanizing in human nature," as he called his efforts in behalf of Sunday Schools, spread rapidly across Britain and was of primary importance in shaping the reading public during the first half of the nineteenth century.[1]

From 1785 until Kay-Stuttleworth became active as secretary of the "Committee of the Privy Council for Education" after 1839, Sunday Schools provided the most effective system of education in Great Britain. Moreover, until the Elementary Education Act of 1870, Sunday Schools probably played a major role in teaching the British masses to read and write. For an age when surveys were inexact, educational statistics often mislead; but in 1818 a parliamentary committee showed that 452,817 English children were educated at Sunday Schools, while 478,849 were educated at unendowed day schools and another 165,433 at endowed schools. The number at Sunday Schools becomes even more impressive when one realizes that unendowed day schools were often run by incompetent teachers like Mr. Wopsle's great aunt in *Great Expectations*.[2]

Sunday Schools were particularly widespread among the lower classes, who could not afford to send their children to unendowed schools or were unable to spare them from work on any day other than Sunday. In May 1816 the "Select Com-

1. John Richard Green, *History of The English People* (London, 1880), IV, 273–274. John James Wright, *The Sunday School: Its Origin and Growth* (London, 1900), p. 3. J. Henry Harris, *Robert Raikes: The Man and His Work* (Bristol, 1900), pp. 15, 23, 215.

2. "A Digest of Parochial Returns Made to The Select Committee Appointed to Inquire into the Education of the Poor: Session 1818," *Parliamentary Reports* (1819), III 224, or *1171, *1275, *1450. For Wales the figures were 7,625 in endowed schools, 22,976 in unendowed schools, and 24,408 in Sunday Schools. In Scotland the totals were 64,338 in endowed schools, 112,187 in unendowed schools, and 53,449 in Sunday Schools.

mittee on the Education of the Lower Orders of the Metropolis" reported its findings. In Spitalfields, a working-class district, it was found, for example, that 110 children attended the parish school, 150 the parish Sunday School, 100 the Protestant Dissenting School, 500 the Methodist Sunday School, 200 a Sunday School in Hope Street, and 800 the Sunday School attached to "Mr. Evans's chapel." These were free, and another 100 children paid two pence a week to go to Mrs. Buxton's School. This pattern was repeated throughout the poorer areas of London. In the Shoreditch district, for example, 160 children were educated in day schools in contrast to 2,069 in Sunday Schools. At Bethnal Green, 130 attended day schools, while 2,405 went to Sunday School.[3]

Robert Raike's school in Gloucester was not the first Sunday School in England. Almost 120 years earlier, the Reverend Joseph Alleine, for example, had started a school in Bath. However, out of step with the spirit of the age and receiving little publicity, these first schools existed in isolation until they died. In contrast Raikes was the proverbial right man at the right time. "The beginning of this scheme," he wrote, "was entirely owing to accident." Some business having led him into the heart of Gloucester "where the lowest of the people" lived, he "was struck with concern at seeing a group of children, wretchedly ragged, at play in the street." Lamenting "their misery and idleness" to an old woman, he learned they were worse on Sunday when they were "all given up to follow their inclinations without restraint, as their parents, totally abandoned themselves, have no idea

3. *Parliamentary Reports* (1816), IV, Pt. 2, pp. 11–13, 104, 123.

of instilling into the minds of their children principles, to which they themselves are entire strangers." Shocked by what he saw, Raikes took matters into his own hands and found four neighborhood women who taught children to read. Paying them each a shilling a Sunday to teach reading and the church catechism to children from ages 6–12, Raikes then discovered a "worthy clergyman" willing to examine the students. Being owner and printer of the *Gloucester Journal*, Raikes printed books for the children and persuaded friends in the Society for Promoting Christian Knowledge to donate testaments and Bibles. Within three years Raikes' Sunday Schools were teaching between 200 and 300 children and "increasing every week." In these first Sunday Schools writing was not taught, and reading lessons themselves were often informal at best. In 1800 a former student recalled fondly how "Winkin' Jim" had disrupted lessons by turning a young badger loose in the school.[4]

More important than the quality of the lessons themselves was Raikes's success in publicizing "this effort at civilization." After interesting local clergymen in the Sunday Schools, Raikes inserted a paragraph in the *Gloucester Journal,* describing the schools. This notice was copied into papers in both London and the provinces. As a result letters of inquiry were sent to the mayor of Gloucester. In replying to one from a Colonel Townley in Sheffield, Raikes described the origin, operations, and success of his plan in some detail. In turn this letter was published in 1784 in the *Gentleman's Magazine*, which promoted Sunday Schools as something of

4. Wright, p. 7. *Gentleman's Magazine,* 54 (1784), 410–412. Harris, p. 40.

a minor cause. "It is with great pleasure," the *Magazine* declared, that "we give place to this benevolent plan; which promises fair to transmit the name of Mr. R. Raikes to later posterity." The following year, William Fox, a London merchant and deacon in a Baptist Church, wrote Raikes to find out if children could learn to read by attending school one day a week. Not only did Raikes answer yes, but he added that the schools had excited in the children's parents "a desire to gain further instruction." Encouraged by Raikes, Fox became the primary mover in organizing the "Sunday School Society." Founded on 7 September 1785, and consisting of a president, four vice-presidents, a secretary, a treasurer, and a committee of twenty-four composed equally of members of the Established Church and Protestant Dissenters, the Society met the second Wednesday in January, April, July, and October. Enthusiasm was not wanting; within one year over a thousand pounds had been subscribed for promoting the Schools.[5]

With the founding of the Society, Raikes fell from view. As the grand old man of the movement, numerous tributes were paid to him; but the work of spreading Sunday Schools was now in other hands. Indicating how quickly the concept of Sunday Schools spread, the two most prominent British periodicals that reviewed literary, cultural, and scientific works were now swamped with publications on Sunday Schools. Late in 1785 the *Monthly Review* discussed two sermons on Sunday Schools. Of one preached before the Archdeacon of

5. *Gentleman's Magazine*, 54 (1784). 412. *The Sunday School Jubilee* (London, 1831), pp. 16–17. William Turner, *Sunday Schools Recommended* (Newcastle, 1786), pp. 57–60.

Rochester, the *Review* wrote that "no well-disposed person will read it without being a friend to the design." So others might learn how to establish similar schools, the journal described the financing of Rochester's schools and pointed out the suitability of Sunday Schools for manufacturing districts in which children worked six days a week.[6]

The *Critical Review* was slower to climb on the bandwagon. In March 1786 it wrote that it was "much inclined to wish success" to the movement. By November, however, it had fallen in line with popular opinion. There was little doubt, the journal wrote, that "the common people" would "be rendered better servants, more able assistants, and more useful members of society" if they were instructed in their duty and learned to read reflectively. Not content merely to approve the schools, the journal defended the movement against the widespread belief that the health of children, particularly those employed in "manufactories," would be impaired by taking away their day of exercise and relaxation. Thinking this objection was "in a great degree visionary," the *Critical* suggested that cleanliness could "certainly supply the defect" of exercise. Besides defending Sunday Schools against this weak but nevertheless frequently heard criticism, the journal discussed the conduct of several schools and favorably concluded that all were "successful in reforming both the manners and the dispositions of the children."[7]

By 1786 Sunday Schools were thriving in places as diverse as Leeds, Rochester, Canterbury, Manchester, Birmingham,

6. *Monthly Review,* 73 (1785), 319–320.
7. *Critical Review,* 61 (1786), 230; 62 (1786), 363–365.

Shrewsbury, and London. More importantly, prominent members of the Church of England declared their support for and adduced strong arguments in favor of the schools. In 1786 Beilby Porteus, Bishop of Chester, soon to be Bishop of London, published *A Letter to the Clergy of the Diocese of Chester*, in which he contrasted Sunday Schools favorably with Charity Schools and argued that the spread of Sunday Schools could lead to a reformation of manners. With the Gordon Riots possibly in mind, Porteus declared: "The extreme depravity and licentiousness . . . among the lowest orders of the people" made Englishmen unsafe even in their homes. Jails were overflowing, and the severe penal code did not deter crime. For Porteus religious education was not only everyone's duty but also the only remedy for the chaos threatening society. Although Charity Schools had been founded with the best intentions, they could be "nothing more than *partial* and *local* remedies." The expense of their founding and maintenance prevented them "from becoming *universal.*" Moreover, there were no Charity Schools in a great many towns and cities. Even in London where they were widely established, Porteus wrote, they took in but "a very small part of the children of the poor." The rest were left, Porteus continued, "to themselves without education, without instruction in the great duties of morality and religion, without any good principles or virtuous discipline to counteract the corruption of their nature, the growth of their passions, the temptations of the world, and the bad examples they too often" saw "at home." Unlike Charity Schools, the bishop wrote, Sunday Schools could be established in villages. Citing the example of Manchester in which there were already 37 schools, 73 teachers, and 2520 scholars, he showed that expense could be kept to a minimum. Typically a teacher with twenty pupils received a shilling a Sunday. Allowing forty shillings a year for books and rewards, the total expense for twenty pupils for a year's education was only four pounds, twelve shillings.[8]

Another early champion of Sunday Schools was George Horne, Dean of Canterbury and later Bishop of Norwich. Like Porteus, Horne buttressed his support for Sunday Schools with two arguments. First, true Christianity taught man that he had a moral responsibility for others. Second, since "monthly scenes" were exhibited in England which "would shock the minds of Turks and Tarters," it was in England's self-interest that Sunday Schools be propogated as a cure-all for the ills of society. "Dark as the prospect was," Horne wrote of England's future, "a ray of light has broken in upon it, and that from an unexpected quarter. An institution has been set on foot by a private individual [Raikes], to the excellency of which every man who loves his country must rejoice to bear his testimony." Following Porteus' pattern, Horne praised the relative cheapness of Sunday School education and then estimated that there were at least 100,000 students in Sunday Schools and predicted that soon there would be ten times that number. In passing he also demolished an argument that was gaining currency in strict evangelical circles: that Sunday School teachers were Sab-

8. Beilby Porteus, *A Letter to the Clergy of the Diocese of Chester* (London, 1786), pp. 5–7, 28.

bath breakers. Horne pointed out that if this were true, then so were "the ministers of religion throughout the Christian world."[9]

Published support for Sunday Schools was not limited to the south of England and the Established Church. Before the annual meeting of the "Associated Dissenting Ministers of the Northern Countries" in June 1786, William Turner preached a sermon entitled *Sunday Schools Recommended.* Like Porteus and Horne, Turner pointed out the inadequacy of Charity Schools. Similarly he estimated that more than 100,000 children were already being educated in Sunday Schools and predicted if the schools spread over the country "at least five times as many may soon reap the benefit." Although Turner's and Horne's enthusiasm carried them too far and their figures were high, their visions were clear. Within the next decade the number of Sunday scholars grew so rapidly that 500,000 seems a reasonable estimate. An accurate count of the number of Sunday scholars is impossible to obtain. The number increased geometrically rather than arithmetically. Initially encompassing but a small minority of schools, the Sunday School Society in January 1788, for example, estimated that 333 schools with some 21,000 students were affiliated with their organization. By April 1789 the estimate had risen to 590 and 39,298, respectively.[10]

9. George Horne, *Sunday Schools Recommended* (Oxford, 1786), pp. 3–4, 14.

10. Turner, p. 24. Sarah Trimmer, *Reflections upon the Education of Children in Charity Schools* (London, 1792), p. 13. Joshua Toulmin, *The Rise, Progress, and Effects of Sunday Schools* (Taunton, 1789), p. 16.

If Robert Raikes was the founder of the movement, then Sarah Trimmer was its first leading theorist and most successful publicist. Indeed, after excepting Hannah More, the *British Critic* wrote of Mrs. Trimmer in 1802 that they could not "name a female author, whose attention to the subject of education, and whose zeal in the cause of charity, have so effectually tended to adorn the character of her sex, and to promote universal benevolence." Born in 1741 Mrs. Trimmer was the daughter of Joshua Kirby, who taught perspective to the Prince of Wales, later George III. As a young woman her range of acquaintance was large. Not only had she known Dr. Johnson and Gainsborough, but she was on friendly terms with many members of the aristocracy, something that helped make her influential when she became interested in Sunday Schools.[11]

After reading Mrs. Barbauld's *An Easy Lesson for Children* in 1780, Mrs. Trimmer wrote *Easy Introduction to the Knowledge of Nature*, the design of which "was to open the minds of children to a variety of information, to induce them to make observations on the works of nature, and to lead them up to the universal Parent, the Creator of this world and of all things in it." After the publication of the *Easy Introduction*, Mrs. Trimmer, who had twelve children, single-mindedly devoted her extrafamilial energies to promoting the education of children and the lower classes. In an age of crusading and prolific authors, she stood almost alone in moral vigor. When the Sunday School movement began, she became a whole-hearted supporter, founding her own schools

11. *British Critic,* 19 (1802), 22–23.

in Brentford and writing many influential works both about and to be used in Sunday Schools.[12]

Mrs. Trimmer did not have an original mind. Instead she was a synthesizer, gathering current ideas on education and weaving them into a coherent fabric. Her most important work on Sunday Schools was *The Œconomy of Charity.* Published in 1787, the book quickly ran through three editions, and in the opinion of Mrs. Trimmer's biographers (Her Children, 1814), "no publication on this subject was of more utility." Illustrating the influential support the Sunday School movement had acquired, the book grew out of an interview Mrs. Trimmer had with Queen Charlotte. Hearing of Mrs. Trimmer's successful schools at Brentford, the Queen asked her for suggestions on how to found similar schools in Windsor. Realizing that "a book of general information upon the subject might save trouble" and at the same time be the means of inducing people to undertake Sunday Schools, Mrs. Trimmer wrote *The Œconomy of Charity.*[13]

Dedicated to the Queen, the *Œconomy* was primarily addressed "to persons in the middling stations of life," in particular "ladies" who would be moved to found Sunday Schools out of moral *noblesse oblige.* For Mrs. Trimmer, the spread of Sunday Schools would lead to a general reformation of manners. "We have now the happiness to see the gospel, the 'Grain of mustard seed',", she wrote enthusiastically, "the growth of which has been so long obstructed by the pernicious weeds of impiety and profligacy, shooting

12. Her Children, *Some Account of the Life and Writings of Mrs. Trimmer* (London, 1814), I, 43.
13. Ibid, pp. 47–48.

forth its branches to different parts of the kingdom, and thousands, nay hundreds of thousands, taking shelter under them against the evils of ignorance and vice."[14]

With her opinion, like that of Horne and Porteus, formed by the Gordon Riots, Mrs. Trimmer believed that England teetered on the edge of chaos, if not revolution. The class structure had become stratified. Latitudinarian charity had not broken down barriers between people, and as a result there was little communication between the rich and the poor. "The higher and middle ranks," she wrote, "are so refined, and the lower so vulgar, that their language is in many respects as unintelligible to each other as if they came from different regions of the world." Under the banner of Christianity, Sunday School scholars would unite "this divided country."[15]

Although humanitarians, the founders of Sunday Schools were not democrats, and to a great extent the phenomenal success of the movement stemmed from its anti-egalitarianism. The upper and upper middle classes became Sunday School patrons because they thought such institutions would make the hierarchial structure of society more stable. If poor children were "lifted from the dunghill, decently clothed, and noticed by their superiors," Mrs. Trimmer thought, the moral quality of English life, not the structure of society, would be changed. Embracing the idea that the child was the father of the man, founders of the movement carefully taught their scholars the "rightness" of their humble places in life. In her abridgment of *Sunday School Dialogues*, meant

14. Trimmer, *The Œconomy of Charity* (London, 1787), pp. vi, 2, 23.
15. Ibid., pp. 11, 14.

to be used as the basis of Sunday study, Mrs. Trimmer included instructive pieces on the structure of society. The dialogue on poverty, for example, revealed the movement's basic conservatism. Mary, a small child, having asked why some people were poor if God loved them, the teacher answered "because God knows best what is proper for every one: this I am sure of, poor people will go to Heaven when they die, if they live good lives; and then they will no longer be poor and distressed, but as happy as if they had been rich." Moreover, there were advantages to being poor, the teacher continued, for poor men could plow ground, dig gardens, and drive carts, things which rich men did not have the strength to do. Likewise, unlike rich women, poor women could clean houses and wash and iron. Not satisfied with this answer [as well she might not be], Mary persisted and asked why poor people had to "do these things any more than the rich." Mixing religious concepts of duty with the vague "fitness of things" and sentimental primitivism, the teacher replied, "because God placed them in a low station, and made it their duty to do so. It is no such hardship to be poor, *Mary*, as many people are apt to think, for good people always find friends to help them in time of need; and when they are well, working gives them health and spirits." Evoking charity not so much as the rationale for good deeds but as support for toleration of the oligarchic structure of society, the teacher told Mary that if she were charitable she would be as happy as if she "had all the riches in the world." Discontent and envy not only made "poor people unhappy" but led to damnation. "Be sure, *Mary*," the teacher warned, "to keep from discontent and envy; for they will make you more wretched than you can possibly imagine. God will not love you, your fellow creatures will despise you, and you will not be fit to go to Heaven when you die."[16]

To the modern mind, such statements are uncongenial. But it is unfair to criticize the founders of the Sunday School movement for what they were not or—if the art historian Wölfflin is correct in believing "even the most original talent cannot proceed beyond certain limits which are fixed for it by the date of its birth"—for what they could not be. Although thinking that the general adoption of Sunday Schools would lead to a reformation of manners, the early supporters of the movement did not believe in any sort of Godwinian universal benevolence. Universal benevolence was a fine ship, as Sydney Smith put it, so long as there were people to take care of the particular duties of setting the sails and pulling the ropes. The first leaders of the movement were forced to take care of particular duties. Finding it hard to believe "that so much ignorance existed out of Africa," they were so busy teaching the poorer classes the virtues of religion and cleanliness and the skills of reading and writing that they had little time for abstractions.[17]

Not only was the *Œconomy* an apologia for Sunday Schools, it was also a practical handbook for prospective patrons and teachers. Besides information on Sunday Schools,

16. Ibid., p. 46. Trimmer, *Sunday School Dialogues: Being an Abridgment of a Work by M.P.* [Eleanor, Lady Fenn] (London, 1790), pp. 19–23.

17. D. W. Robertson, *A Preface to Chaucer* (Princeton, 1963), p. vii. *Edinburgh Review,* 1 (1802), 21. Arthur Roberts, ed., *Mendip Annals: or, A Narrative of the Charitable Labours of Hannah and Martha More* (London, 1859), p. 51.

details were included on how to finance and establish schools of industry "so that poor girls could learn how to spin, card wool, or do needlework." Suggestions were made on how to establish an Evening Navigation School for boys living in villages near the sea. The Sunday School day itself was divided into morning and evening sessions, each lasting anywhere from two to four hours. In the morning session, children repeated morning prayer, spelled, read scriptural histories, and learned the church catechism. In the evening or afternoon session, students said evening prayer, read the Bible, spelled, and listened to lectures. The higher classes read moral and religious works, including religious tracts and the *Sunday School Dialogues*. The lectures themselves were usually on broad doctrinal subjects such as "The Nature and Attributes of God" or were moral sermons on virtuous living such as "Duty to Neighbors," "Duty of Loving Brothers and Sisters," "On Stealing," "On Chastity," and "Of Inoffensiveness."[18]

Although Mrs. Trimmer did not make provisions for writing or arithmetic, most schools eventually taught both, particularly to boys. There was, however, a great deal of controversy about teaching these subjects. Purists held that as practical skills writing and arithmetic were not fit subjects for schools "designed to put people in the way of attaining the KINGDOM OF HEAVEN." On the other hand, reading gave the poor "a *proportionate* share of of learning," enough so they could be "partakers of the great national blessing of having an ENGLISH BIBLE." During the Napoleonic Wars, when edu-

18. Trimmer, *Œconomy*, pp. 58 ff. See also Trimmer's *The Sunday School Catechist* (London, 1788).

cation came under fire from conservatives, teaching practical subjects was criticized as being "eventually hurtful both to the children themselves and the nation at large." "For labourers of the lower classes, particularly in the country," the *Anti-Jacobin Review* wrote, "this surely is unnecessary. Without *really* improving their mind, it, *at least* gives them a *fancied* superiority, and renders them unfit for their occupations. Let the precepts of virtue and religion rather be orally impressed on their memory, than that their minds should be confused by a smattering of letter learning. It is not by the mere knowledge of reading, writing, arithmetic, algebra, or geometry, that a man becomes moral or religious."[19]

With thousands of schools administered in varying degrees of efficiency by numerous patrons and a score of denominations, it is impossible to assess the quality of Sunday School education. Starting from the minimal assumption that some education was better than no education, we can, however, reach tentative conclusions. We know, for example, from the parliamentary testimony of 1816 that students usually took two to three years to learn how to read. Since many children started when they were six and others working in "manufactories" had little time to devote to studies, this does not seem an unreasonable length of time. Moreover, we can deduce from the number of readers turned out that reading, at least, must generally have been well taught. The numbers of new

---

19. Trimmer, *The Sunday School Catechist*, pp. 2–3. Trimmer, *A Comparative View of the New Plan of Education Promulgated by Mr. Joseph Lancaster . . . and of the System of Christian Education* (London, 1805), p. 127. *Anti-Jacobin*, 9 (1801), 389–390.

readers must always remain speculative, but on their strength, Hannah More began the *Cheap Repository Tracts,* two million of which were sold for distribution to the poor during a one-year period and which had a monumental effect on the reading public in the early nineteenth century. A similar concern led to formation of the Religious Tract Society in 1799. Fifty years later, with greatly expanded horizons, the Society had published 500 million copies of tracts and books in 110 languages and dialects. Early in the nineteenth century, however, it declared modestly, "the general extension of education also renders it an imperative duty upon christians to be more active than they have hitherto been, lest the talent of reading, which they have communicated as a blessing, should be abused and rendered a curse." The number of new readers gave impetus not only to tract societies but also to periodicals, including *The Cottage Magazine, or Plain Christian's Library* (1812) and *The Evangelical Magazine* (1793). In the preface to the first volume, the *Evangelical Magazine* made clear that Sunday scholars formed a large part of its prospective audience, writing, "Thousands read a Magazine, who have neither money to purchase, nor leisure to peruse, large volumes. It is therefore a powerful engine in the moral world, and may, by skilful management, be directed to the accomplishment of the most salutary or destructive purposes. And its influence must increase in proportion to the increase of schools for instructing the poor, which are becoming so numerous, that probably, a few years hence, it will be a rare thing to find a beggar in the land who has not been taught to read." Fifteen years later, the *Evangelical Magazine* had the largest circulation of any English journal, almost twice that of the influential *Edinburgh Review*.[20]

The spread of Sunday Schools led to an increased emphasis on children's education, not only in the lower classes but also in the growing middle classes. In 1779 and 1781 Anna Barbauld published her *Lessons for Children* and her *Hymns in Prose for Children* respectively. In large print with spaces between lines and paragraphs, these works were designed "*to impress devotional feelings as early as possible on the infant mind . . . to impress them by connecting religion with a variety of sensible objects; with all that he* [a child] *sees, all he hears, all that affects his young mind with wonder or delight; and thus by deep, strong, and permanent associations, to lay that best foundation for practical devotion in future life.*" Among the first books adopted for use in Sunday Schools of all theological hues, Mrs. Barbauld's works help set the pattern for children's books for the next fifty years. By 1785 John Marshall already had a list of some 65 children's books, a great many of which were modelled on Mrs. Barbauld's and written by Mrs. Trimmer, Lady Eleanor Fenn, and Dorothy and Mary Ann Kilner.[21]

20. *Parliamentary Reports* (1816), IV, Pt. 2, pp. 12, 16. *Mendip Annals*, pp. 6–7. William Jones, *The Jubilee Memorial of the Religious Tract Society* (London, 1850), p. vi. *An Address to Christians on the Distribution of Religious Tracts*, Religious Tract Society (London, 1805), p. 8. *The Cottage Magazine*, 1 (1812), iii. *Evangelical Magazine*, 1 (1793), preface.

21. Anna Barbauld, *Hymns in Prose for Children* (London, 1781), pp. v–vi. The Marshall list is attached to the British Museum's copy of A.C.'s *The Footstep to Mrs. Trimmer's Sacred History* (London, 1785).

These children's books were inspired not only by a belief in the crucial importance of an early and structured education but also by a distrust of sensibility. As early as 1785, the *Monthly Review* praised a "modern" children's tale, Mary Ann Kilner's *The Adventures of a Pincushion* and contrasted it favorably with earlier children's tales of sensibility. "The little volumes of the nursery," the *Monthly Review* wrote, "are no longer filled with the nonsensical fables of witches, hobgoblins, and Jack the Giant-killer, which formerly disgraced even the *Children's* libraries. The monsters and fairies, and other products of old-wivery, now give way to the realities of common life, and the dictates of common sense." The rejection of children's tales of wonder or sensibility was so widespread that by 1802 Charles Lamb's sister Mary had trouble finding the "old classics" at Newbery's bookstore. According to Lamb, the shopkeeper "hardly deigned to reach them off an old exploded corner of a shelf" while "Mrs. B's and Mrs. Trimmer's nonsense lay in piles about." "Science," he wrote Coleridge, "has succeeded to Poetry no less in the little walks of children than with men. Is there no possibility of averting this sore evil? Think what you would have been now, if instead of being fed with Tales and old wives' fables in childhood, you had been crammed with geography and natural history? Damn them! —I mean the cursed Barbauld Crew, those Blights and Blasts of all that is Human in man and child."[22]

22. *Monthly Review,* 72 (1785), 469. E. V. Lucas, ed., *The Letters of Charles Lamb: To Which Are Added Those of His Sister Mary Lamb* (London, 1935), I, 326.

In 1877 Mrs. Barbauld's biographer wrote enthusiastically about the *Hymns* asking rhetorically, "Where, in the long catalogue of children's books, shall we find any to be compared with them? Many who heard them the first time at their mother's knee can trace to them their deepest, most precious convictions. A century has now passed since they were written; they have been largely used by all classes from the palace to the cottage, and still what a freshness and beauty in every page!" Even after allowance has been made for biographical afflatus, this was a remarkable tribute. More importantly, it was repeated throughout the century. In his implied approval of sensibility and disgust for "educational" children's literature, Lamb was "all, all alone." In the literary world, Fanny Burney, William Hazlitt, William Wordsworth, and Samuel Coleridge testified to Mrs. Barbauld's influence; and for Henry Crabb Robinson, meeting Mrs. Barbauld was like meeting the Angel Gabriel.[23]

In 1802 the *Guardian of Education* recounted the history of children's books in England, paying particular attention to the fall of sensibility and the rise of morality. Before the reign of Queen Anne, the *Guardian* wrote, there were few children's books. During and after Queen Anne's reign, *"the first period of Infantine and Juvenile Literature"* began. During this time, Mother Goose's Fairy Tales, Aesop's and

23. Jerom Murch, *Mrs. Barbauld and Her Contemporaries* (London, 1877), p. 75. Charlotte Barrett, ed., *Diary and Letters of Madame D'Arblay* [Fanny Burney] (London, 1905), V, 419. P. P. Howe, ed., *The Complete Works of William Hazlitt* (London, 1930), V, 147. Thomas Sadler, ed., *Diary, Reminiscences, and Correspondence of Henry Crabb Robinson* (London, 1869), I, 225–226. Earle Leslie Griggs, ed., *Unpublished Letters of Samuel Taylor Coleridge* (London, 1932), I, 45, 102.

Gay's Fables, and *The Little Female Academy* by Mrs. Fielding were prominent. "In general of a very harmless nature," these books "were mostly calculated to entertain the imagination, rather than to improve the heart or cultivate the understanding." With the founding of Newbery's library and with Mrs. Barbauld's "introducing a species of writing, in the style of *familiar conversation,* which is certainly much better suited to the capacities of young children than any that preceded it," the present period of religious literature for children began. "These useful hints given by Mrs. B." the journal continued, were "generally adopted by her cotemporaries, and many books have been supplied to the nursery, by means of which children at an early age have acquired the rudiments of useful science, and even of the first principles of Christianity, with delight to themselves, and ease to their instructors."[24]

What the specific influences of Mrs. Barbauld or of the children's literature, spawned by the Sunday School movement were is impossible to ascertain. Certainly, though, if we accept the premise which the late eighteenth and early nineteenth centuries accepted, that the child is the father of the man, then the foundation of much of what we think of as Romantic or Victorian was strongly influenced by the Sunday School movement. "It cannot be doubted," Dr. Johnson's friend Anna Seward wrote, "that the understanding, and virtue, the safety, and happiness of those branches of Society which are raised above the necessity of mechanic toil, depend much upon the early impressions they receive from books which captivate the imagination, and interest the heart."

24. *Guardian of Education,* 1 (1802), 62–64.

According to Priscilla Wakefield "the universality of Sunday Schools" was "likely to produce a visible alteration in the manners of the peasantry." The next generation of "labouring poor" was certain to be "more civilized than their predecessors."[25]

Although the initial supporters of the Sunday Schools believed that a reformation of manners had to "be begun among the young," they hoped that children would inspire their parents to better themselves. Typical was the tale told by the secretary of the Hoxton Academy, a London Sunday School with 560 pupils, a circulating religious library, and Monday evening classes in writing and arithmetic—all for only seventy pounds a year. In one family, the secretary said, a young girl took home a tract and read it to her mother. "The father, who was in the practice of spending the whole of his Sunday at a public-house" overheard the girl reading, and as a result said he would go to the chapel. "Since that time," the secretary recounted, the man had "been in the habit of attending a place of worship instead of the public-house." In the first years of the movement, countless versions of this inspirational tale were told throughout England. Clearly though this indirect brand of adult education was not satisfactory on any large scale. And it was just a matter of time until Sunday School supporters broadened their concerns and devoted some of their energies to adults. Again Mrs. Trimmer was the effective national leader. In 1786 she wrote *The Servant's*

25. Anna Seward, *Variety* (London, 1788), p. 213. Priscilla Wakefield, *Reflections on the Present Condition of the Female Sex: With Suggestions for Its Improvement* (London, 1798), p. 191.

Friend, an Exemplary Tale: Designed to Enforce Religious Instructions Given at Sunday and Other Charity Schools. With its companion piece, *The Two Farmers,* this biography of poor but honest Thomas Simkins was an 86,000-word novel. A saga of virtue rewarded, *The Servant's Friend* painstakingly exposed the wages of sensibility in susceptible laborers and chambermaids.[26]

Written not only for the highest Sunday School form but also for cottagers and servants for whom there were few moral narratives "blending entertainment with instruction," *The Servant's Friend* was extremely popular. Eventually it became part of the list of the Society for Promoting Christian Knowledge when the Society tried to lure lower-class readers away from "the hot-bed of a circulating library" and out of earshot of peddlers selling licentious ballads.[27]

In terms of her career and the future of the novel, however, *The Servant's Friend* merely prepared Mrs. Trimmer for writing the most significant work of the decade. Lasting only two years (1788–89), the monthly *Family Magazine* was, nevertheless, a seminal journal. Aimed, like *The Servant's Friend,* at cottagers and servants, it was a miscellany containing "matter which had a tendency to improve and

26. Turner, p. 18. *Parliamentary Reports* (1816), IV, Pt. 2, p. 156. The tract the father overheard his daughter reading was Legh Richmond's *The Dairyman's Daughter.*

27. Hannah More, *Strictures on the Modern System of Female Education* (London, 1799), I, 160. *An Address to Christians Recommending the Distribution of Cheap Religious Tracts,* Religious Tract Society (London, 1799), p. 11. All future references to *An Address* will be to this edition.

lead the mind to religion and virtue" and sound politics. Each number contained a sermon, short, didactic essays on topics such as "the Pernicious Effects of Dram-Drinking," fables, moral poems, descriptions of the habits of animals, practical hints on gardening and household skills, xenophobic accounts of foreign countries in which care was taken "to make the lower orders see the comforts and advantages belonging to this favored land," and current events moralized: sensational accounts about everything from highway robbery to the sinking of an India merchantman and from boxing to the execution of pirates.[28]

By far the most significant part of the magazine was the monthly "Instructive Tale." In the first issue of the journal Andrews, a conscientious country squire, found many able-bodied men intoxicated in The George, a local inn. Succeeding numbers described how Andrews with the help of his wife steered the men back to the paths of virtue. As the Andrewses visited the men's homes, a series of tales followed; they were entitled, typically, "The Notable Daughter," "The Jealous Wife," "The Generous Blacksmith," and "The Unexpected Reformation." In homespun fashion each tale taught a moral truth. Moreover, the same characters appeared throughout, so that by the last tale the community became an instructive microcosm of what England was and what she could be. Literarily the stories were poor stuff, but since Mrs. Trimmer and Hannah More were close friends, it seems likely that the tales provided the pattern for the form and substance of the *Cheap Repository Tracts*. Indeed Hannah More

28. *Some Account,* I, 49–50.

viewed Mrs. Trimmer's ability "to write so much" as a "tacit reproach" and as late as 1791 hesitated even to mention her name after that of Mrs. Trimmer. *The Cheap Repository* changed the hesitancy, however, and to many minds these *Tracts*, not Pitt's repressive domestic policy, prevented a revolution on the French model from occurring in England. Discussing the influence of the *Tracts*, the *Evangelical Magazine* said in 1809 that it was to Mrs. More's pen that "the world, in its different ranks, owes perhaps greater obligations than to that of any other living author." To my mind these obligations were not so much political as they were literary.[29]

Although there will always be doubt over whether Mrs. Trimmer's "Instructive Tales" provided the pattern for the *Cheap Repository,* Mrs. More herself said that the founding of Sunday Schools and a consequent awareness of the educational and moral deficiencies of the lower class led to the *Tracts*. In the 1790's Hannah More replaced Mrs. Trimmer as the most important author, patron, and publicist of the Sunday School movement. Becoming interested in Sunday Schools in 1789, Hannah and her sister Martha opened their first school in October in a village they called "our little Sierra Leone." Like Mrs. Trimmer the Mores wanted "to form the lower class to habits of industry and virtue." Their curriculum read like Mrs. Trimmer's, with the prayer book, Bible, and church catechism forming the moral core. With the financial backing of Henry Thornton, who had been treasurer of the Sunday School Society, and William Wil-

29. *Evangelical Magazine,* 17 (1809), 289. *Some Account,* I, 281–283.

berforce, leader of the anti-slavery forces in the House of Commons, the Mores, by July 1793, were the patrons of nine schools attended by nearly 1,000 children.[30]

If it had not been for the Napoleonic Wars, Hannah More would probably not have become the emblematic leader of the Sunday School movement and subsequently the most influential British writer of fiction of her day. But as Henry Cockburn recalled, however, "everything, not this or that thing, but literally everything, was soaked in this one event." Thinking that the French were emulating Britain's own bloodless constitutional revolution of 1688, British liberals greeted the Revolution enthusiastically. Charles James Fox exclaimed, "How much the greatest event it is that ever happened in the world! and how much the best!" Samuel Romilly said that all men, even if they were not liberal or philosophical, joined in sounding the praises of the Parisians and celebrating an event so important for mankind. As the bloodless revolution became violent, however, this initial Foxite enthusiasm for an oppressed people's reenacting the Glorious Revolution of 1688 did not last. Soon members of Parliament were calling France the vilest of nations, governed by a gang of robbers and cut-throats. Jingoism spread across

---

30. *Mendip Annals*, pp. 6, 43. Henry Thompson believed that Mrs. Trimmer interested Hannah More in Sunday Schools. *The Œconomy of Charity*, he wrote, was "a work addressed to ladies, with which it is impossible to suppose Mrs. More unacquainted." It was impossible, he continued, for her not to have been impressed "by its simple eloquence of plain facts and clear deductions" and it was "highly probable" that she inspected Mrs. Trimmer's "establishments herself." Henry Thompson, *The Life of Hannah More: With Notices of Her Sisters* (London, 1838), p. 90.

Britain, reaching a peak immediately after the beheading of Louis XVI. Fox's nephew Lord Holland noted that "the impression made upon the publick by the execution of Louis XVI. was so deep and so universal, that an Englishman was hardly permitted, in publick or in private, to express any opinion on politicks, without first pronouncing an anathema against the French Convention." When Britain went to war with France, a wave of bellicose patriotism swept the country. Homes of leading liberals were burned. In Scotland, Judge Braxfield transported reformers on flimsy grounds, holding that the Constitution was perfect and that anyone who supported change advocated *de facto* revolution. In 1794 *habeas corpus* was suspended. Criticism of the government was construed to be criticism of the British way of life. Thinking that the Crown was destroying British liberties, the Whigs seceded from Parliament; and Fox remarked pessimistically to Howick, the future Lord Grey of the Reform Bill of 1832, "opposition seems to be out of the question, perhaps forever; and we may boast . . . that we were the last of the Romans." Fox's pessimism proved unwarranted: four years later the Whigs formed a ministry. But his statement indicated the extent to which antijacobinism pervaded English life.[31]

Fearing that liberal notions derived from France would

---

31. Henry Thomas Cockburn, *Memorials of His Time* (Edinburgh, 1856), p. 80. Lord John Russell, ed., *Memorials and Correspondence of Charles James Fox* (London, 1853–57), II, 361; III, 368. Samuel Romilly, *Memoirs of the Life of Samuel Romilly* (London, 1840), I, 356. *Parliamentary History*, 30 (1792), 81, 111. Henry Richard Lord Holland (afterwards Vassall), *Memoirs of the Whig Party during My Time* (London, 1852), I, 28.

undermine the Constitution, Tories were forever finding jacobinical tendencies among all reformers. This was especially true in education, where a strong parliamentary group supported measures which, they said, inhibited the importation and spread of "French poison." Arguing that the French monarchy had been overturned by the press, they believed that jacobinical conspiracy was trying to corrupt the lower classes by spreading seditious writings. Fear of seditious writing led to an anti-educational attitude based on the identification of ignorance with patriotism. Fuel was added to that blaze by Thomas Paine, whom conservatives identified with the devil. "A nation under a well regulated government," Paine wrote in the *Rights of Man* (1792), "should permit none to remain uninstructed. It is monarchial and aristocratical government only that requires ignorance for its support." Such writings, conservatives stated, were *"proper objects"* for *"the hangman's faggots"*; and innumerable pamphlets were published warning Britons against Paine's "baneful, abominable, infectious, and corrupting breath." In his *Moral View of Society* the Tory polemicist John Bowles explained the link between education and jacobinism. Jacobins, fiends in human shape, he wrote, did not war against arts and sciences but instead supported education and strained all the faculties of the mind to the greatest degree of exertion. Indefatigably they explored nature's secrets and carried civilization's refinements to the utmost improvement. But these accomplishments, Bowles argued, only rendered them a more grievous scourge to humanity. Their talents and knowledge better enabled them to pursue their destructive projects and made them more likely to attack religion and government and establish their sway of vice and impiety.[32]

At the same time that doubt over the wisdom of educating the lower classes was spreading, the Church of England swung sharply to the theological right, with the result that latitudinarianism became generally discredited. Those "motions of compassion" that had been the hallmark of the Christian now indicated a *"profligacy of sentiment"* equalled only by "the more gross expressions" which occurred in the age of Charles II. In *A Tale of the Times* (1799), Mrs. West wrote that "the unchristian morals of the present strain their affected charity till they embrace vice, while the most glaring enormities are glossed over by delicate subterfuges; and refined liberality expatiates on the goodness of the heart, while its possessor breaks every precept in the decalogue." Simplistically broad church theology became equated with Socinianism and its denial of original sin, the atonement, and the Trinity. Although they were not sure exactly what Socinians were and called them infidels, Turkish Christians, and avowed enemies of Christ, conservative Britons were positive that Socinians threatened the Constitution by subverting the Church. Burke assured Parliament that unless Socinians were stopped, they would destroy all British institutions and

32. *Parliamentary History,* 29 (1792), 1478; 30 (1793), 541, 728, 732. Thomas Paine, *Rights of Man* (London, 1792), Pt. II, p. 131. Francis Oldys, *The Abridged Life of Thomas Pain* (London, 1793), advertisement. Isaac Hunt, *Rights of Englishmen. An Antidote to the Poison Now Vended by the Transatlantic Republican Thomas Paine* (London, 1791), p. 8. John Bowles, *A View of the Moral State of Society at the Close of the Eighteenth Century . . . and Continued to the Commencement of the Year 1804* (London, 1804), p. 5.

would rebuild the state on a French model encompassing Tom Paine's doctrines. Even in the cooler days of 1815, the *Anti-Jacobin* published a letter from "Amicus Patriae" which blamed the Napoleonic Wars on Socinianism and Jacobinism. "Influenced solely by the public *spirit* every Man owes his Country," Amicus wrote, "I resolved the first opening that offered, to attack the whole Infidel Tribe of Preachers and Orators, the sympathising twin brothers Socinianism and Jacobinism." "The effects of Socinianism, and its twin brother," he concluded, "are to be found in revolutions, in the overthrow of empires, in treasons, strategems, and spoils."[33]

With this general rejection of broad church theology came the particular rejection of the belief that a religion of mere charity would create a more stable society. In biblical terms, New Testament ethics of love yielded to Hebraic law. Doctrine, Clarke's "Worm at the Root of *Jonah's* Gourd," particularly the doctrine of original sin, became all important as both theologians and politicians preached the necessity of "positive laws" for keeping man's "evil propensities . . . from breaking forth" and for upholding those "ancient rules . . . taught by divine wisdom."[34]

33. Mrs. Jane West, *Letters Addressed to a Young Man, on His First Entrance into Life, and Adapted to the Peculiar Circumstances of the Present* (London, 1801), III, 186; *A Tale of the Times* (London, 1799), II, 6. *Socinian Blasphemy Exposed, or the Confutation of Error and the Triumph of Truth* (London, 1789), pp. 8, 10. *Socinianism Unmasked* (London, 1790), p. 2. *Parliamentary History*, 29 (1792), 1381–1395. *Anti-Jacobin*, 48 (1815), 84–86.

34. William Wilberforce, *A Practical View of the Prevailing Religions of Professed Christians in the Higher and Middle Classes* (London,

Despite the reservations of some conservatives who thought sectarianism *de facto* jacobinism, the evangelical movement gathered even more momentum as greater numbers of people became convinced that only Old Testament law could control "the perverted and depraved . . . faculties of the mind." In "an age of infidelity," the *Arminian Magazine* warned, "something more is wanted than the alphabet of religion." Only "those pure lights" of true faith could "dissipate the clouds of modern philosophy, and the darkness of corruption."[35]

As might be expected, the conservative reaction to the French Revolution accelerated what had been the novel of sensibility's gradual fall from favor. No longer was broad church theology the source of the man of feeling. No longer were Richardson, Brooke, and MacKenzie praised for bringing tears to "those eyes that love to shed the sacred drops of sympathy." Instead Rousseau was held responsible for the novel's excessive sentiment. As "the first popular dispenser of this complicated drug," Rousseau, Hannah More wrote, created characters who practiced "superfluous acts of generosity" while "trampling on obvious and commanded duties." Combining "inflated sentiments of honour with actions the most flagitious," Rousseau's heroes and heroines taught that no duty existed which was "not prompted by feeling" and that impulse was "the main spring" of virtuous action while law and religion were only "unjust restraints." In 1798 the

---

1797), p. 32. Bowles, *Reflections on the Political and Moral State of Society at the Close of the Eighteenth Century* (London, 1800), p. 127.

35. *Evangelical Magazine,* 2 (1794), 21. *Arminian Magazine,* 15 (1792), 17.

Anti-Jacobin printed a cartoon by James Gillray entitled "New Morality." In the corner of the drawing stood three hags on platforms. With daggers in both hands, her foul bosom exposed, snakes in her hair, and her foot on a knife, Egalité stood over justice. Above philanthropy and on papers entitled "Ties of Nature" and "Amor Patriae" loomed a grotesque fat woman who bit the North Pole while she squeezed the world out of shape. Lastly, above Sensibility and on the crowned head of a king stood a figure who wept over a dead robin in her right hand while clutching Rousseau's works in her left.[36]

The cartoon illustrated how far the reputations of Rousseau and sensibility had fallen in Britain. Rousseau's initial popularity had coincided with the popularity of sensibility and is interesting for the indirect light it sheds upon British attitudes toward the novel and sensibility. First appearing in England in 1760, Rousseau's *Eloisa* was an immediate success. The novel's stress upon the goodness of man and implicit denial of original sin smacked of Clarke's Pelagianism. Julie's use of the heart as a guide, rather than heart-breaking rules of society, appealed to readers who thought Christianity was more a matter of spirit than rules and institutions. Filled with melancholy scenes, threats of suicide, and rivers of tears, the book evoked motions of compassion. Moreover, Wolmar was Tillotson's Christian with a kind and obliging disposition and a tender and compassionate spirit. Like Scott's ideal Christian, he was "ready to every good Work,

36. *London Magazine*, 38 (1769), 438–439. More, *Strictures*, I, 31–34. *Anti-Jacobin*, 1 (1798), illustration.

and like Fields of Spices" scattered his "Perfumes through all the Neighbourhood."

When *Eloisa* appeared in translation, leading English journals compared Rousseau to Richardson. In particular, comparisons were drawn to *Clarissa,* which Dr. Johnson had said was "not only the first *novel,* but perhaps the first *work* in our language, splendid in point of genius, and calculated to promote the dearest interests of religion and virtue." For the *Critical Review* Rousseau was an "ingenious author, spirited and masterly in all his productions." Indeed "the highest encomium" that could be bestowed on Richardson was that he had "been deemed worthy the imitation of Rousseau's eminence." In their critique of the book, the *Monthly Review* took occasion to defend the novel as a genre, writing, "we confess our difference in opinion from those who consider all romances merely as books of amusement. It is certainly in the power of a moral, sensible writer, to convey instruction in any form or guise he shall think fit to assume; and, considering the prevailing taste of the present age, we know not whether, as a novelist, his lessons are not most likely to command attention."[37]

For the leading English journals of the 1760's, Rousseau was the archetypical moral and sensible writer, whose novels were filled with lessons on religion and education. Praising *Emilius and Sophia,* the *Critical Review* wrote that they were "pleased with that moral sense of right and wrong" which Rousseau discovered "implanted by the hand of nature in the

37. *Variety,* p. 215. *Critical Review,* 12 (1762), 203–204. *Monthly Review,* 24 (1761), 227.

minds of infants." Anticipating critics who might attack Rousseau because of his "natural religion," the *Monthly Review* took a broad church stance, writing, "our author is, indeed, the most zealous Advocate for Toleration; and if he sometimes bears hard on the mere forms of religion, he tells us plainly, it is because they are destructive to the spirit of it." As Clarke condemned rigid Christian ceremony and doctrine, so the *Monthly Review* criticized contemporary methods of educating children. Believing that *Emilius* taught the proper spirit of education, if not the spirit of Christianity, the journal repeated and seconded Rousseau's arguments for "natural education."[38]

In the different climate of 1791, Rousseau was no longer an admired sentimental theorist. Instead he was the philosopher behind the Revolution. In *A Letter . . . to a Member of the National Assembly,* Edmund Burke at once summed up and determined Rousseau's reputation during the Napoleonic Wars. According to Burke, books recommended by public authority soon formed the character of an age. This was especially true in France, where the National Assembly recommended Rousseau to the nation's youth. Moreover, the leaders of the Assembly jealously disputed which among them best resembled Rousseau. "In truth," Burke wrote, "they all resemble him. His blood they transfuse into their minds and into their manners. Him they study; him they meditate; him they turn over in all the time they can spare from the laborious mischief of the day, or the debauches of the night. Rousseau is their canon of *Polycletus*; he is their standard of per-

38. *Critical Review,* 14 (1763), 258. *Monthly Review,* 27 (1762), 215.

fection." At Rousseau's feet, Burke wrote, could be laid the responsibility for the Revolution. "By the false sympathies" of *Eloisa*, he undermined the family, the building block of the nation. Moreover, his irregular life, Burke held, illustrated the evils of a universal benevolence which neglected particular duties. A charge that could be leveled unfairly at almost any philosopher, this was a telling blow, not simply because of the glaring discrepancy between Rousseau's life and thought. Thinking that their own society had become so stratified that there was dangerously little communication between the rich and the poor, Britons believed that benevolent acts rather than abstract philosophy offered the best antidote for the diseased revolutionary state of the nation.[39]

To remedy this, many tracts were written which preached the virtues of active benevolence and the dangers of abstract philosophy. In Hannah More's *The History of Mr. Fantom, the New Fashioned Philosopher and His Man William*, Mr. Fantom was an anglicized Rousseau, who neglected his responsibility for individuals while he planned to relieve "the miseries of the whole world" once the reign of universal benevolence began. Not only did he think the church "a superstitious prejudice," meant only "for the vulgar," but he despised "the man whose benevolence" was "swallowed up in the narrow concerns of his own family, or perish, or country." As Rousseau had neglected his family, so Mr. Fantom paid little attention to his household. Moreover as Rousseau's philosophy, so Britons thought, had led to the moral deter-

39. Edmund Burke, *A Letter from Mr. Burke to a Member of the National Assembly* (London, 1791), pp. 30–35, 43.

45

ioration of the French lower classes and ultimately to the revolutionary bloodbath, so Mr. Fantom's philosophy led to the moral and physical destruction of his servant William. Overhearing his master expound his theories, William became, in effect, the child of Rousseau's thought. First he stopped attending church; next he stopped praying; and since, as he later recounted, "this gave satan great power over me," he was soon far along the road to damnation. Discharged by Mr. Fantom for drunkenness and theft, he eventually became a murderer. The moment of truth came, however, for Mr. Fantom and those among Hannah More's readers who had philosophic leanings when in the company of Mr. Trueman they visited William's prison cell. There they learned that the paths of philosophy led but to the scaffold. "You are the cause," William told Mr. Fantom, "of my being about to suffer a shameful death." "From you," he declared, "I learnt the principles which lead to those crimes. By the grace of God I should never have fallen into sins deserving of the gallows if I had not often overheard you say there was no hereafter, no judgment, no future reckoning."[40]

Burke's criticism was but the first of many attacks by prominent conservatives on Rousseau. In 1793 Thomas Rennell, one of Pitt's stalking horses, followed in Burke's footsteps, writing that "the mischief done to morality and religion by this man are beyond all calculation. The passions in their worst excesses are painted by him in the garb of virtue, and by this means the progress made in vice is most art-

---

40. Hannah More, *The History of Mr. Fantom, the New Fashioned Philosopher, and His Man William*, Cheap Repository Tracts (London, 1798?), pp. 8, 12, 19, 21.

fully rendered imperceptible to the unwary mind. Conscience is subverted, and mock principle, a thousand times worse than none, is substituted in its place. The purest philanthropy is the profession of this writer; but the real purpose and effect of his writings is to diffuse a principle of sentimental profligacy, and canting libertinism." Rennell's criticisms were echoed in kind throughout the decade, most prominently by William Wilberforce in his *Practical Christianity* (1797) and John Bowles in his *Reflections on the Political and Moral State of Society at the Close of the Eighteenth Century* (1800).[41]

Hyperbole became so much the rule of Rousseau criticism that by the end of the century Rousseau was a demonic mythological figure. Not surprisingly, Mrs. Trimmer founded the *Guardian of Education*, primarily to expose the pernicious influences of Rousseau on children's literature and education. The first number of the journal stated baldly "the greatest injury the youth of this nation ever received, was from the introduction of Rousseau's system, given to the world in the history of *Emilius*, an imaginary pupil, educated upon an entirely new principle; which proposed to banish Christianity from the nursery and the school, to make room for a *false Philosophy*, which has no foundation in truth or reason." After reading Rousseau, the journal contended, many parents raised their children without a knowledge of religion. This led to a general decline in religion and undermined the structure of society. Instead of giving children

41. Thomas Rennell, *The Connexion of the Duties of Loving the Brotherhood, Fearing God, and Honouring the King* (London, 1793), p. 2.

"the natural liberty of the mind," the *Guardian* urged the "unspeakable advantage" of laying the "only true foundation of morals" in childhood. "Nothing," the *Guardian* argued, could "more effectively guard society and individuals from *crimes*" than "implanting in them the salutary fear . . . of the common Father and Judge of all Mankind."[42]

Not content merely to warn readers about Rousseau's "false Philosophy," the *Guardian* printed long critiques of *Emilius* and *Eloisa* which ran through several issues. Readers were urged to be on guard against Rousseau's "deistical tenets." "Sentimental wickedness," the journal wrote, is "infinitely more dangerous than sensual. Satan when clad in a mild cherubic form deceived (as our great Poet, Milton, has finely imagined) *Uriel, the sharpest-sighted spirit of all in Heaven,* and obtained admission into Paradise." Clearly Rousseau was just such a Satanic figure, sentimentally making a heroine out of a prostitute and rendering a child "averse" to "the laws both of God and Man."[43]

As went the reputations of Rousseau and sensibility, so went the reputation of the novel, particularly among religious readers. For the *Eclectic Review* the mischief a novelist could cause was limited only by the powers of his genius and the principles of his audience, whom the journal advised to stay away from novels. The *Methodist Magazine* held that novels were "like the poisoned shirt presented to Hercules, a pestilent treasure." In *An Address to the Public from*

42. *Guardian of Education,* 1 (1802), 10–11, 375; 2 (1803), 145, 329.
43. Ibid., 1 (1802), 79–80, 138, 141, 185–186. These criticisms were taken primarily from Mrs. West's *Letters Addressed to a Young Man.* See Vol. III, pp. 186–187, 199–200.

the Society for the Suppression of Advice, John Bowles (?), declared: "Infidelity and Insubordination, fostered by the licentiousness of the press, have raised into existence a pestilent swarm of *Blasphemous, Licentious and Obscene Books and Prints,* which are insinuating their way into the recesses of private life, to the destruction of all purity of sentiment, and all correctness of principles. On its "Spiritual Barometer," running from — 70, Perdition, to + 70, Glory, the *Evangelical Magazine* put "Love of Novels" at — 40 with "Scepticism," and "Deistical company prized." "Morality," *The Sylph* wrote, "aims at the government of the passions, and the wise restriction of those propensities of the heart, the uncontrolled indulgence of which leads to misery and guilt. Novels, on the other hand, encourage those propensities, generate and promote a corruption of the manners; and, under the pretence of following nature, take off that curb from the passions which reason and religion would impose."[44]

Contrary to expectation, however, the mounting criticism of education and sensibility did not have an immediate effect upon Sunday Schools. Moreover from the publications written for Sunday Schools would come "novels" which contributed to the genre's regaining respectability in the second decade of the nineteenth century. That Sunday Schools themselves were not immediately effected by the xenophobic fear of education resulted primarily from the national stature

44. *Eclectic Review,* 1 (1805), 60. *Methodist Magazine,* 24 (1801), 386. Bowles (?), *An Address to the Public from the Society for the Suppression of Vice* (London, 1803), Pt. I, p. 43. *Evangelical Magazine,* 18 (1800), 526. *The Sylph,* 1 (1796), 35.

attained by Hannah More and her *Cheap Repository Tracts*. In the 1770's Hannah More had been the friend of Johnson, Garrick, and Reynolds among others. In the mid-1780's she became more interested in religion, becoming intimate with both Horne and Porteus and in 1788 publishing *Thoughts on the Importance of the Manners of the Great to General Society*. Appealing to the upper classes, this popular essay stressed that reform of English morals and manners should filter down from a reformation of the upper classes, rather than arise democratically from the spirit of the people. The anti-egalitarian bent of the essay made Mrs. More many friends in conservative circles, and this friendship was cemented in 1793 when she published an anti-French tract entitled *Village Politics*, supposedly by Will Chip, a country carpenter. Teaching the evils of French "philosophy" and the virtues of Tory politics and the Church Establishment, the tract was remarkably popular, and thousands of copies were printed and sent to Scotland and Ireland in order to counteract the effects of jacobinical propoganda.

After the publication of *Village Politics*, many Britons, including Porteus, now Bishop of London, urged Mrs. More to write other works to counteract the effects of seditious books supposedly being distributed among the poor. Influenced by Porteus and convinced that "to teach the poor to *read*, without providing them with safe books" was "a dangerous measure," she approached her Anglican friends at Clapham. The result was the *Cheap Repository Tracts*, the philosophy of which was summed up in a letter she wrote to Horace Walpole: "from liberty, equality, and the rights of man, good Lord deliver *us!*" Aimed at, in the Claphams' words, the numbers which "have lately been taught to read by means of Sunday Schools," three *Tracts* were published each month. One was a "useful subject versified"; another was "particularly adopted for perusal on the Lord's day"; and the third and most popular type was a moral tale, following the didactic pattern set by Mrs. Trimmer's "Instructive Tales." Initially financed by the Thorntons, 114 *Tracts* selling at ½d, 1d, and 1½d, with cheaper rates for bulk buying, were published for distribution among the poor. With two million sold in a year, their success was phenomenal.[45]

Nothing could have been better suited to soothe the suspicious breasts of antijacobians and show that the leaders of the Sunday School movement were true Britons, teaching right religion and sound politics. Many of the *Tracts* were Pollyanna tales illustrating virtue rewarded and evil pun-

45. William Roberts, *Memoirs of the Life and Correspondence of Mrs. Hannah More* (London, 1834), II, 294, 345 ff., 357. *Mendip Annals,* p. 6. *Evangelical Magazine,* 3 (1795), 388–389; 5 (1797), 170–172. The *Tracts* received much influential support. During the first year of publication, the list of subscribers to the *Cheap Repository* included William Pitt, the Archbishop of Canterbury, and the Bishops of Bath and Wells, Bristol, Chester, Durham, Exeter, Ely, Gloucester, London, Lincoln, Salisbury, and Worcester. The two largest contributions listed were both for 20 pounds. One of these donations was from Samuel Whitbread, a Whig liberal and a member of the wealthy brewing family; the other was the "produce of the Reading Sunday School Play for 1795." For more information see the yearly statement by the *Repository's* treasurer Henry Thornton, published in the one-volume collection *Cheap Repository for Moral & Religious Publications* (London, 1795).

ished. Diligent Dick, Little Jem the chimney sweep, and Betty Brown the St. Giles orange girl all reaped dividends from the home virtues of honesty, loyalty, and integrity. In contrast Black Giles the poacher and Tawney Rachel the fortune teller met unhappy ends. Still other tracts were parables describing the fatal effects of drink, gambling, and seduction. More importantly, though, a large number of the *Tracts* had political overtones. *The Shepherd of Salisbury Plain*, Mrs. More's most famous tract, consisted of didactic discussions between a gentleman farmer and a poor but honest shepherd. Holding that poverty should not be cause for discontent, since Jesus was poor, the shepherd was satisfied with his home even though rain streamed in through the roof. His daughter Molly thought the family wealthy because they had salt for their Sunday meal of water, potatoes, and coarse bread. At the end of the tale, the virtuous shepherd was made village clerk, given a new house with a sound roof, and assured that his family would have plenty of meat. So that Sunday School readers would not miss the message, Mrs. More furnished a coda. At the conclusion the shepherd advised all working men what to do when they were approached by reformers. "When those men who are now disturbing the peace of the world, and trying to destroy the confidence of God's children in their Maker and their Saviour," the shepherd said, "came to my poor hovel with their new doctrines and their new books, I would never look into one of them; for I remembered it was the first sin of the first pair to lose their innocence for the sake of a little wicked knowledge; besides *my own Book told me—To fear God and honour the king—To meddle not with them who are given to change—Not to speak evil of dignities—To render honour to whom honour is due.*"[46] The social and political impact of the *Tracts* was incalculable. According to the *Christian Observer*, the *Cheap Repository Tracts* were "among the mighty barriers that, under God, checked the growth of infidelity and anarchy" in Britain at "the commencement of the French Revolution." For our purposes, however, the possible political influences of the *Cheap Repository* are not so important as the literary ones.[47]

In 1879, Anthony Trollope, after he had become the grand old man of the Victorian novel, published an Olympian essay on the poetics of the novel. For Trollope the novel had "in great measure taken the place of sermons." Girls became wives; wives, mothers; boys grew into manhood in accordance with the morality promulgated by novels. As a result the novelist "must have his own system of ethics" and "preach his sermons with the same purpose as the clergyman." By Trollope's rigorous moral standard, Defoe, Sterne, Fielding, and Smollett were measured and found wanting. In contrast Trollope praised Scott for his "conviction of his duty as a teacher" and called Richardson the "inventor of the modern English novel" because his works improved "those for whom he was writing." Mr. B's boudoir, however, was a long way from the towers of Barchester and even further from Captain Cuttle and the Wooden Midshipman. Certainly Richardson has a prominent place in the history of the novel, but by Trollope's time, Richardson's influence had run a bit thin.

46. More, *The Works of Hannah More* (London, 1801), V, 50.
47. *Christian Observer*, 12 (1813), 390; 15 (1816), 786.

The roots of the Victorian novel and Trollope's moral poetics were a good deal more homespun and popular, in that
they touched more people.[48]

That the novel "in great measure" took the place of sermons resulted from Hannah More and her followers. The
Cheap Repository and their countless progeny not only
helped form the literary taste of the growing reading public
but also determined the shape of the early Victorian novel.
On the simplest level, the moral tales among the *Cheap Repository* were short novelistic parables, illustrating the rewards of virtuous living. Since issues of right and wrong
were clear-cut, the dramatis personae of the stories were, in
Forster's terms, "flat characters." To Hannah More's mind
as to the mind of religious readers and later novelists, characters should be simple generic devices for teaching morality.
In 1809 the *Christian Observer* praised such characters: "they
are principally employed to exemplify or illustrate the precepts which are inculcated; as a father, in an evening walk
with his son, diversifies the conversation by remarks on the
objects around him." Likewise a good book, the *Guardian of
Education* argued, gave "Virtue its own feature" and "Vice
its own image." In contrast the rounded or mixed character
led people astray and "gilded the gallows" by confusing "the
identity of vice and virtue." Put simply, good novels were
modeled on "the parables and allegories of the Divine In-

48. Anthony Trollope, "Novel-Reading," *The Nineteenth Century,* 5
(1879), 24–43. In the first years of the nineteenth century, even Richardson's reputation was tarnished. "His most finished characters," the
Eclectic Review said, were "to be regarded as amiable moralists, not
as well instructed christians." *Eclectic Review,* 1 (1805), 127.

structor of mankind." "The most perfect instances on record of the use of fiction disjoined from all its bad properties," these parables avoided "adorning vice as to make her attractive." Following this moral tradition, Dickens' characters were usually clear-cut embodiments of vice and virtue, so much so that part of the moral force of his novels resulted from readers' easily recognizing the elemental conflicts of good and evil.[49]

Convinced that poetics which smacked of Rousseau were dangerous, Hannah More avoided sensibility. Telling sad or happy, but not moving, stories of parish nurses, good stepmothers, unfortunate gamesters, and honest publicans, the *Tracts* taught that Christian rigor led to happiness and conversely that the wages of sin were always paid. However, since religious journals had relied heavily on "motions of compassion" in describing dying Christians or the special providence of God, Hannah More did not completely avoid sensibility. In particular she often made children her central characters. Behind her use of children lay the example of the divine child. More immediate, though, were scores of statements addressed to Sunday Scholars. According to Mrs. Trimmer, for example, whoever wanted to reach the kingdom of Heaven had to *"humble himself, and become, like a good little child, willing to learn and ready to obey."* In her *Novels of the Eighteen-Forties,* Kathleen Tillotson wrote that "to put a child at the centre of a novel for adults was virtu-

49. E. M. Forster, "Flat and Round Characters," *The Theory of the Novel,* ed. Philip Stevick (New York, 1967), pp. 223–231. *Christian Observer,* 8 (1809), 110, 788; 11 (1812), 782. *Guardian of Education,* 1 (1802), 79, 133.

ally unknown when Dickens wrote *Oliver Twist* and *The Old Curiosity Shop.*" Well before Dickens' novels, however, the use of children as central characters had become a hackneyed convention of religious publications. In the *Cheap Repository* and scores of other tracts, dying Little Nells ferried weaker souls to the promised land. Or, as William Jones put it in the *Jubilee Memorial* of the Religious Tract Society, "who can calculate the numbers that have been safely guided to the rest of the righteous by 'The Dairyman's Daughter' and 'The Young Cottager'?" Like Florence Dombey, Hester Wilmot was the means of saving the souls of her hard-hearted parents. At the end of her story, Hester, a schoolteacher, was the center of an old-fashioned redemptive order like Florence. Cheeks that ran wet over the misfortunes of Oliver Twist had so long since been furrowed by innumerable accounts similar to that of Poor Eliza, a prize Sunday School scholar. Eliza's treasure was her Bible, which she had been given as a reward for "proficiency in reading and recitation of Scripture." Always "subject to asthmatical affection," Eliza breathed her last (and readers wept) when her parents encouraged her sister to become a prostitute. Even the way for Little Nell's pietistic wanderings over England had been prepared for by "the walking Bible," an extraordinary lad who had much of the Bible by heart.[50]

50. Trimmer, *Sunday School Catechist*, p. 3. Kathleen Tillotson, *Novels of the Eighteen-Forties* (Oxford, 1961), p. 50. For Hester Wilmot see *The History of Hester Wilmot; Or, The Second Part of the Sunday School* in the *Cheap Repository*. *Sunday School Gleanings* (London, 1823), p. 37. *Christian Observer*, 23 (1823), 104.

The womb of religious publications was pagan in its fecundity. Not only did it nourish the child-hero, but it also produced the intruding narrator. In *The Twentieth Century Novel*, Joseph Warren Beach stated that pure fiction evoked "a moving picture of life itself." For Beach the outstanding development in technique since Henry James's time was that the story should tell itself, "being conducted through the impressions of the characters." "It is this," Beach wrote, "which finally differentiates fiction from history and philosophy and science." Accordingly authorial commentary on the story was "an empty and perfunctory substitute for the real thing" and reduced "the dramatic tension, the illusion of life." Nurtured on Jamesian poetics, most twentieth-century critics and authors have agreed with Beach, and in 1950 Bradford Booth met little opposition when he argued that the most significant change between Victorian and modern fiction was "the disappearance of the author." As a result of the wide acceptance of Jamesian standards, critics have generally viewed authorial intrusion as a flaw in the Victorian art of the novel. To do so, however, is to misunderstand the moral poetics which lay behind such authorial intrusion.[51]

In the nineteenth century two separate literary traditions supported authorial intrusion. The first, the offspring of *Tristram Shandy*, ran through the novels of Bulwer, Marryat,

51. Joseph Warren Beach, *The Twentieth Century Novel* (New York, 1932), pp. 14–24. Bradford Booth, "Form and Technique," *The Reinterpretation of Victorian Literature*, ed. Joseph Baker (Princeton, 1950), p. 79.

Meredith, and Trollope. Characterized by Sterne-like playfulness and learned wit, this tradition rested firmly on the association of ideas, found in Locke's *Essay Concerning Human Understanding*. For our purposes, the other, and stronger, tradition is more important. Hannah More and her followers thought Sterne an unreadable member of the School of Rousseau. According to Wilberforce, Sterne had abused his god-given talent of being able to "touch the finest strings of the human heart." Instead his writings vitiated "that purity of mind, intended by Providence as the companion and preservative of youthful virtue."[52]

In contrast to Shandyists, religious writers intruded themselves into their narratives—not to call attention to themselves as narrators, but to underline the didacticism of their stories. Furthermore their "*first, great* object was to instruct," not to create "the illusion of life." Believing that such an illusion of life was bad for lively imaginations, moral writers consciously forced readers out of imaginary worlds. Positing a student-teacher relationship between author and reader, narrative intrusions focused attention not on the art of, but on the didacticism of, the novel. In describing the misfortunes of Little Jem, the chimney sweep, the author intruded into the narrative to preach a short sermon and assure readers that goodness would win out. "Hitherto," he wrote, "we have seen virtue oppressed, and vice apparently triumphant;

52. Wilberforce, pp. 282–284. For more on the Shandy-tradition of authorial intrusion, see my " 'The Most "Harum-Scarum" Sort of Novel We Have Ever Encountered': Marryat's 'The King's Own' And Shandyism," *English Studies in Africa*, 17 (1974), 70–77.

but let the good rest assured, that in the end they shall
not go unrewarded; and let the wicked consider, that should
they for a time escape the punishment of their evil doings,
the hour of death is approaching, which they cannot avoid,
that then the severest vengeance will over take their
crimes."[53]

In 1799 in their initial tract "An Address to Christians
Recommending the Distribution of Cheap Religious Tracts,"
the Religious Tract Society listed the qualities to be found
in a successful tract. Along with *"Pure truth"* was the re-
quirement that a tract should be "so plain that it cannot
possibly be misunderstood." Accepting this at face value, a
generation of tract and novel writers addressed their readers
directly in order to ensure that no one would miss a story's
main point. Consequently, to bring Trollope back to mind,
the novel in great measure took the place of sermons. The
disappearance of the author in the latter half of the nineteenth century is another matter; but it is, I think, linked to
the decline of widely accepted objective (Christian) standards of right and wrong.[54]

The Victorian novel's debt to religious writings and particularly those occasioned by the Sunday School movement

---

53. *Christian Observer*, 8 (1809), 115. *Sweep, Soot O!*, Cheap Repository tracts (London, 1798?), p. 17. In *The Infidel Father* Mrs. West
happily explained to her readers that if she occasionally intruded into
the narrative, it was "either from a wish to gratify the curiosity of the
public, by giving them a peep behind the curtain, or to illustrate some
important truth by a familiar incident, a method which people of
superior genius often have recourse to" (I, 12–13).

54. *An Address*, pp. 10–11.

was not limited to content or technique, but embraced a matter so fundamental as form. In *The English Common Reader*, Richard Altick stated that when Chapman and Hall "first laid plans for the book that became *The Posthumous Papers of the Pickwick Club*," they had in mind a picture book issued in parts, "the sort of thing that had become popular with William Combe's *Dr. Syntax's Tours* (1812–21) and Pierce Egan's *Life in London* (1820–21)." After the phenomenal success of the *Pickwick Papers*, issuing new fiction in parts became a popular form of publication until the 1870's, with Dickens, Lever, Thackeray, and Trollope issuing many of their novels in monthly numbers.[55]

Dickens and Chapman and Hall did not originate publication of new fiction in parts. More important than Egan's and Combe's picture books were the influence and example of religious tracts. Particularly significant was the ubiquitous *Cheap Repository*. Although most of the stories in it were complete in a single tract, several were published in parts. With a frontispiece for each part and often ornamented with crude woodcuts, some of the stories resembled short, illustrated novels. Thus, for example, *The Two Shoemakers* was some 25,000 words long, and *The Two Wealthy Farmers* was over 35,000 words. The stories that were divided into only two parts usually appeared in consecutive months. For the longer tales, however, there was no established publication pattern. The first part of *The Two Shoemakers* appeared in 1795, while the last three parts and a related "Sunday Reading" tract which contained the religious thoughts of

55. Richard Altick, *The English Common Reader* (Chicago, 1963), p. 279.

the "good" shoemaker James Stock were not published until
1796. Publication of *The Two Wealthy Farmers* was even
more erratic, its seven parts appearing over a three-year
period. Distributed not only through Sunday Schools but
also by hawkers who could use publication by parts to attract
and hold their readers, and by men like the Reverend Samuel Kilpin, who in the early nineteenth century was not satisfied unless he gave away 10,000 publications a year, tracts
were often the only "godly" fiction available to the lower
classes.[56]

The specific effects of this distribution upon the Victorian
reading public's acceptance of part-issue must always remain
speculative. But since most early Victorians learned to read
in Sunday Schools, where tracts resembling those of the
Cheap Repository were the primary reading material, the
Victorian's ready acceptance of part-issue in the 1830's may
have reflected their Sunday School education.

In any case, the *Cheap Repository* was not only the source
of part-issue, but also the begetter of hordes of imitators.
When the danger of a British version of the French Revolution appeared unlikely, Hannah More and her friends
stopped publishing the *Cheap Repository*. Their success,
however, inspired other groups with religious axes to grind.
In 1799 the Religious Tract Society was founded. By 1823
the Society had published 51 millions of tracts. Although the
Society's list included sermons, doctrinal treatises, handbills,
and broadsheets, instructive tales were its most important
type of publication. In their declaration of intent, the Society
showed that it had learned narrative technique from the

56. Jones, p. 173.

Cheap Repository. "A plain didactic essay on a religious subject," the Society declared, "may be read by a christian with much pleasure; but the persons for whom these tracts are chiefly designed, will fall asleep over it ... There must be something to allure the listless to read, and this can only be done by blending entertainment with instruction. Where *narrative* can be made the medium of conveying truth, it is eagerly to be embraced." Consequently among the Society's initial publications were the first numbers of Rowland Hill's *Village Dialogues.* With accounts of Farmer Littleworth, Mr. Lovegood, and Mr. Worthy continuing from number to number, the Village Dialogues copied the technique and content of the *Cheap Repository.* By 1824, long after the Religious Tract Society had parted ways with Hill's bilious Calvinism, the twenty-fourth edition of the *Dialogues* appeared.[57]

Hannah More's imitators were not restricted to England. In Ireland Mary Leadbeater published her *Cottage Dialogues among the Irish Peasantry,* fifty-four tracts which followed the fortunes of frugal, hard-working Rose and Jem and the misfortunes of vain and irresponsible Nancy and Tim. In reviewing the *Cottage Dialogues,* the *Christian Observer* noted Mary Leadbeater's debt to Hannah More, writing that the originality of the *Cheap Repository* would "continue a lasting monument, no less" of Mrs. More's "benevolence than of her genius." In Scotland, clergy in Dumfriesshire wrote *The Scotch Cheap Repository Tracts,*

57. *An Address,* p. 11.

modelled on Hannah More's "captivating mode of instruction."[58]

The Religious Tract Society was but one of many tract societies founded in the wake of the *Cheap Repository*. In 1799 the Society for Distributing Evangelical Tracts Gratis was established to promote "the knowledge of divine truth in simplicity" and to stem "the mighty torrent . . . of popery, infidelity, and avowed atheism." In 1804 the British and Foreign Bible Society was founded. The next year the venerable Society for Promoting Christian Knowledge, which had imbibed new life from the *Cheap Repository*, published 112,440 tracts. Lists and statistics often cloud rather than clear the truth; but within a short period, a score of societies and individuals were publishing tracts totalling several hundred thousands annually for the moral benefit of Britons. Zealous individuals bought handfuls and gave them to their neighbors, distributed them on the turnpike, or left them in public houses. In its Second Annual Report, the Religious Tract Society claimed, as might be expected, that "the lives of some persons, and the deaths of others, appear to have been beneficially influenced by the Publications already issued. Such proofs of the Divine Sanction are felt as new bonds of attachment, new motives to gratitude, new impulses to zeal." Religious journals were filled with accounts of tracts directing woe-begotten sinners to the rest of the righteous. Typically a correspondent of the *Evangelical Magazine* urged readers

58. *Christian Observer*, 10 (1811), 238. Mary Leadbeater, *Cottage Dialogues* (London, 1811). *The Scotch Cheap Repository Tracts* (Edinburgh, 1815), p. iii.

to distribute tracts, writing, "At the awful, but glorious day of judgment, when all things shall be made known, how will he that drew the bow at a venture rejoice with him that received the blessed golden arrow dipt in the blood of Jesus!"[59]

Like the effects of children's literature, the effects of this outgrowth of the Sunday School movement are impossible to quantify. But it seems likely that many early nineteenth century attitudes can be traced back to the shaping influence of the Sunday School movement which tried to bind men's days each to each in natural piety. Certainly, though, the *Cheap Repository* set the pattern for the narrative tract and by extension had much influence upon the Victorian novel.

59. *Evangelical Magazine,* 8 (1800), 80; 9 (1801), 452. "Second Annual Report of the Religious Tract Society" (London, 1801), p. 5. The Society for Distributing Evangelical Tracts Gratis was short-lived. Since it appeared that it and the Religious Tract Society "would clash by separate operations," a "cordial union" was effected. See "An Account of the Origin and Progress of the London Religious Tract Society" (London, 1803).

Chapter 2
The Christian Observer and the Novel

The thriving state of tract publishing indirectly indicated the healthy condition of the Sunday School movement. In fact, the movement had just come unscathed through its first trial by fire. For almost two years that Argus-eyed protector of British liberty the *Anti-Jacobin* had strained its polemical energies trying to prove that Sunday Schools "in themselves excellent" had "been grossly perverted by the arts of sectaries, and . . . rendered instruments of hostility to our establishments, both civil and religious." The *Anti-Jacobin's* campaign failed miserably; and by 1802, Sunday Schools were firmly established in the public mind as "the greatest of charities."[1]

Despite their popularity and the almost perfervid belief that distributors of novel-like tracts were imitating "the example of the master," moral criticism of the novel itself had grown stronger. In his *Uncorrupted Christianity*, Thomas Belsham held that "the profession of religion, in some form or other" was "the fashion of the day." For Belsham this religiosity resulted primarily from the wrong cause: "that foul

1. *Anti-Jacobin*, 6 (1800), 228–229. *Methodist Magazine*, 25 (1802), 433.

and groundless clamour, which for political and party reasons was raised some years ago against a neighbouring country, as a nation of atheists and infidels." Be that as it may, religious concerns had a greater influence upon popular criticism of the novel than at any time since the appearance of *Pamela*. Believing that Satan had not labored so hard "to ruin Mankind" since the flood, religious critics rigorously examined the moral implications of novel-reading. Turning a blind eye on tracts, such critics discovered that reading novels was to the mind what dram-drinking was to the body.[2]

In contrast to the novel, critics of literature approved biography. For years biography had been the staple of religious journals. When the *Cheap Repository* first appeared, the *Evangelical Magazine* urged the Claphams to avoid the dangers that lurked "beneath the flowers of fiction" by adopting real facts as the basis of tracts. In 1794 the *Protestant Dissenter's Magazine* defended its heavy focus on biography by asserting that "BIOGRAPHICAL information" was useful and entertaining. In 1800 the *Methodist Magazine* justified its inclusion of biography and clarified the *Dissenter's* meaning of *useful*. "Few subjects, except those immediately of a religious nature," the journal wrote "have a greater tendency to promote humility, benevolence, and piety. The man whose heart is enlarged with LOVE TO GOD, necessarily feels an interest in the concerns of his fellow-creatures; hence arises a desire to know the events which have taken place among men. The man whose heart glows with LOVE TO MAN, will naturally

2. *An Address*, p. 1. Thomas Belsham, *Uncorrupted Christianity* (London, 1811), pp. 3–5. *Guardian of Education*, 3 (1804), 139. Solomon Grildrig, *The Miniature* (London, 1806), p. 28.

be stimulated to beneficient actions, by instances placed before him, of distinguished zeal and industry." Explaining
its policy of not reviewing novels, the *Baptist Magazine*
stated that "the region of fact supplies such combinations of
character, principle, and circumstances, as are fully adequate
to every purpose of moral suasion or spiritual instruction."[3]

In the abstract, the differentiation between fiction and
biography seems simple enough. But in the workaday world
of sectarian periodicals, the differentiation led to intellectual
elephant-swallowing. While condemning novels as the food
of vitiated and sickly imaginations, religious journals published, under the guise of biography, the most sensational
stories that appeared during the age.

Appearing in the *Methodist Magazine* in 1808, the account
of William Andrew Horne was typical of these stories, which
were geared more toward titillating readers' imaginations
than saving their souls. Born on November 30, 1685, Horne
was the eldest son of a landed gentleman in Derbyshire. The
favorite of his father, as a youth he was given money and
horses and "permitted to ramble from one place of diversion
to another." "In this course of dissipation he gave loose to
his passion for women." Not only did he seduce his mother's
maids and supposedly murder a servant girl who was with
child, but he "had criminal intercourse with his own sisters."
In February 1724 his sister having been delivered of a fine
boy, Horne gathered up the baby and asked his brother
Charles to accompany him on a midnight ride. After gal-

3. *Evangelical Magazine*, 5 (1797), 171. *Protestant Dissenter's Magazine*, 1 (1794), 1. *Methodist Magazine*, 23 (1800), 374. *Baptist Magazine*,
4 (1812), 391–392.

loping five miles, Horne dismounted and covered the child up in a haystack. The next morning the boy was dead; and when Charles later told his father about the incident, the old man "insisted he should never speak of it." The night journey remained a secret until 1747, when Horne's father died, aged 102. Charles then went to a magistrate, but the magistrate told him to keep quiet as the affair might hang half the family.

Sometime later Horne threatened a Mr. Roe for killing game. Words arose, and Roe called Horne "an incestuous old dog," for which Roe was prosecuted in Ecclesiastical Court. Unable to prove the charges, Roe was forced to pay expenses. Roe then heard about Charles' earlier visit to the magistrate. When questioned, Charles said the rumor was true. A warrant was taken out. William heard about it and asked Charles to forswear himself. Charles refused, but said if William would give him five pounds, he would emigrate. William refused; and after much legal jocking (no one it seems wanted to try the case), William was brought to trial in August 1759. The same people who had found the child's body were turned up; Charles' evidence was corroborated, and William was convicted and sentenced to be hanged. On the day of his execution he forgave all his enemies, even Charles, but said "that at the day of Judgment, if God Almighty should ask him how his brother Charles behaved, he would not give him a good character." Executed on his seventy-fourth birthday, William went to the gallows regretting only that he had not had time to enjoy his usual birthday treat of plum pudding.

If the mere events of Horne's sin and death were not sensational enough, the journal recounted several anecdotes about his "churlishness." On his father's death, for example, although Charles was left the personal estate, William took twelve guineas out of the dead man's pocket and refused to give them to Charles unless he paid the funeral expenses. Later William turned Charles out of the house and refused to give Charles' children any assistance, so that they were reduced to begging and his brother to keeping "a little alehouse" near the gate of the family estate. At the conclusion of this account of Horne's misdeeds, the writer commented straightforwardly that as there were no more Hornes in Derbyshire, "how appropriate the words of Holy Writ: 'The wicked is driven away in his wickedness. His name shall rot.' "[4]

Although the *Methodist Magazine* was particularly given to printing sensational tales, such stories appeared in all popular religious journals. Not only did they undermine the periodicals' jeremiads against the novel but they also whetted appetites for novels. Similarly tracts accustomed readers to novelistic techniques. Appearing in the *Scotch Cheap Repository*, "The Spoiled Child" was a short novel, showing that novels mingled "poison with entertainment" and corrupted "the safeguards of virtue." Inconsistencies of this sort tied religious journals in critical knots and confused readers.[5]

During the first twenty years of the nineteenth century, the *Christian Observer* changed its critical position on fiction many times. Founded in 1802 by the Clapham Sect, the *Observer* was the most literate of the early nineteenth-century

4. *Methodist Magazine*, 31 (1808), 28–32.
5. *The Spoiled Child*, Scotch Cheap Repository Tracts, p. 144.

religious periodicals. Under Zachary Macaulay's editorship, the journal became something of a pacemaker, articulating critical standards for the novel relatively soon in comparison to other sectarian journals. This was not done, however, without rigorous thought and soul-searching.

After the stock patriotic assurance that the periodical was "conducted upon the true principles of the Established Church," the founders mounted the tub and used the Prospectus to proclaim their high moral purpose. Believing like Josiah Pratt that literature was "the great engine acting upon society," they declared their intentions of becoming critical Cato's, writing: "At a period like this, when Dramatic Compositions, Novels, Tales, Newspapers, Magazines, and Reviews are disseminating doctrines subversive of all morality, and propogating tenets the most hostile to piety, order, and general happiness, some friends of civil government and revealed religion, have felt it incumbent on them openly to oppose the progress of lawless opinions, to strip scepticism and imposture of their artful disguise, and, by displaying the true features of libertinism and impiety, to expose them to deserved contempt and abhorrence."[6]

Behind this alarmist view of literature lay the belief that the novel was the fiefdom of the world, the flesh, and the devil. Although skillful journalistic tightrope walking enabled the periodical to avoid reviewing a "pure" novel until 1809, the *Observer's* eight-section format immersed the magazine in critical inconsistency from the very start. Four of the

6. John A. Pratt, ed., *Eclectic Notes: or, Notes of Discussions on Religious Topics at the Meetings of the Eclectic Society* (London, 1856), p. 13. *Christian Observer,* 1 (1802), iii.

divisions (View of Public Affairs; Select List of New Publications; Intelligence, Literary, Philosophical, etc.; and Religious Intelligence) were straightforward enough. But the other four (Religious Communications, primarily Religious Biography; Miscellanies, mostly correspondence but also Anecdotes and Poetry; Review of New Publications; and Obituaries) often depended on novelistic devices. The people in the *Observer's* biographies and obituaries were regularly fictionalized to fit a didactic pattern. Leaning heavily on tearful but apocalyptic death scenes, the biographies teetered on the abyss of sensibility. Even more novelistic were the didactic characters of females, supposedly written by Hannah More.[7]

Accounts of slavery seemed like chapters from gothic novels. Shocking descriptions of slavery were published in order to create a moral climate favorable to abolition. Although the purpose was noble, the method rested on condemned Socinian "motions of compassion." From Barbados came the horrifying story of the kindly slave who *"touched with compassion for her unfortunate mistress,"* presumed to release her after her husband beat her and locked her in chains. Enraged, the husband forced the slave's tongue through a hole in a board to which he fastened it on the opposite side with a fork. Later deciding he had been too kind, he tore the slave's tongue off near the root. From Demerara, a correspondent wrote about a husband and wife who fled their brutal

7. For Hannah More's characters see *Christian Observer*, 2 (1803), 16 ff. Biographies, travel reviews, and accounts of slavery appear in practically every volume. To avoid a plague of footnotes, I have included the volume and page references in the text.

master. Caught, the husband was murdered in front of his wife, and she was so badly beaten "as to exhibit one extreme sore from the loins almost down to her hams." Going untreated, the wounds became so infected that it took half an hour to pick out all the maggots (IV, 220; V, 371). To drive home Britain's moral duty to Christianize the heathen, the *Observer* reviewed many travel books. Concentrating on the abuses of paganism, these reviews similarly tried to arouse reader indignation with vignettes of sensibility.

The use of novelistic techniques, albeit in a good cause, was a venial inconsistency when compared to the *Observer's* attitude toward tracts. Although the Clapham Sect's own Hannah More "fathered" the contemporary tract, Macaulay reviewed few tracts during the journal's first years. Adopting an "out of sight, out of controversy" position, the *Observer* did not take a strong stand on fiction until 1805. Even then the statement appeared obliquely as a digression in a review on the education of women. After leaving himself a way out by declaring there "possibly might be an exception," the reviewer attacked sensibility, stating that novels gave "a false and distorted picture of human nature." Moreover they vitiated the taste by creating a state of "unnatural excitation" and blunted the "benevolent affections" by encouraging readers "to substitute mere sentiment in the place of conscience and a sense of duty" (IV, 45–46).

In September 1805, however, the *Observer* forsook its critical disdain and rigorously examined the novel. The occasion was provided by the publication of *A World without Souls*, a highly didactic novel by John Cunningham, the curate of John Venn at Clapham Common. Combining three elements: a *Rasselas*-like philosophic tale, Swift's imaginary voyage (highly sanitized), and sermons on morality, the book began with Gustavus, "an ingenuous youth of seventeen" debating with his tutor M——, an Imlac figure of sixty. M—— supported the authenticity of an article which Gustavus had read and which said that there was a tribe of Americans lacking souls. Unable to convince Gustavus, whose sentiments were colored by romance, M—— proposed they leave their Happy Valley among the rocks of St. Foy in Switzerland and journey to the city of O (London).

After telling his fiancée Emily good-bye, Gustavus set out for London with M——. While in England they visited fashionable and evangelical churches, the opera, gaming houses, and the theater. Gustavus saw a duel, heard a debate on slavery in the House of Commons, attended a fashionable marriage, and learned the sad fate of M——'s sister, who had a "diseased sensibility." After these experiences (parables followed by short sermons), Gustavus discovered that indeed there were men without souls. At the end of the book, a wiser and sadder Gustavus fled London and returned to his natural Eden and unspoiled Eve.[8]

Clearly uneasy with *A World without Souls*, the *Observer* hesitated to call Cunningham a novelist and instead stressed his "originality." Although Cunningham found "his niche" among sentimental writers, he was different from Sterne. Instead of appealing to the imagination, *A World without Souls* was "addressed more to the heart." Moreover Cunning-

8. John Cunningham, *A World without Souls* (London, 1805).

ham quit his subject before it degenerated into "rhapsody and whim," and advancing to "a firmer note," vindicated "the cause of truth, virtue, and real religion." In contrast, the *Observer* wrote, it has been the great defect of "our moral sentimentalists" that "the standard of virtue is so low, and their maxims of morality so often false, as to make it doubtful by whom truth has suffered most, its friends or its enemies . . . In fact, *they* have made religion, or rather morality, (the former name it does not deserve), the vehicle of sentiment: with them truth has been subsidiary to feeling." For the *Observer* the novel of sensibility possessed the persuasive powers of smooth-tongued Belial. Imported from France, it had "been too often the source, or channel, of licentiousness." There was scarcely a sentiment which could disgrace human nature, the journal stated, "but when gilded with plausibility of feeling" would not be "greedily swallowed by the unwary." Happily, however, Cunningham overcame the dangers of fiction by forgetting the novelist. Placing the fictional "cone on its right base," he "surmounted religion with sentiment, and made feeling the ornament of truth" (IV, 543–551).

More at home attacking "moral sentimentalists" than praising novels in which feeling was subsidiary to truth, the *Observer* avoided reviewing tracts and novels for two years. In part this reflected a conscious effort by the Claphams to forestall criticism of their evangelical Anglicanism and to avoid being labeled methodists. Applied pejoratively to all evangelicals, the word "methodist" raised specters of jacobinism in the minds of extreme Tories. Hannah More herself was still smarting from the *Anti-Jacobin*'s attacks on the Sunday

School movement, in which she had been called a Calvinist and been compared to a serpent.[9] Trying to establish reputations for stability and patriotism, the Claphams worked hard to convince the public that their brand of evangelicalism was orthodox. Strictly speaking, this was so, but since they supported the anti-slavery movement and missionary activity abroad, it was easy to confuse them with Dissenters. Moreover their theology, with its stress on original sin, the atonement, and salvation by faith was similar in kind to that of "methodistical" dissent. In 1797 William Wilberforce published the Claphams' religious manifesto: *A Practical View of the Prevailing Religious Systems of Professed Christians in the Higher and Middle Classes Contrasted with Real Christianity.* Supposing a theological kinship, evangelical journals reviewed it favorably. "It is with unfeigned pleasure," the *Protestant Dissenter's Magazine* wrote, "that amidst the infidelity, indifference, and dissipation of the age, we see a member of the British senate daring the 'world's dread laugh,' and avowing himself not merely a nominal, but an experimental christian."[10]

Wanting to dissociate themselves from such theological familiarity, the Claphams hesitated to review religious tracts. Praise of evangelical tracts, they realized, would be construed as proof of their methodism. On the other hand, since they approved the didacticism of most imitations of the *Cheap Repository*, they did not want to attack them. The dilemma was insoluble, and the Claphams took the rational way out and "lay low."

9. *Anti-Jacobin*, 9 (1801), 277 ff.; 11 (1802), 423–424.
10. *Protestant Dissenter's Magazine*, 4 (1797), 196.

In part reluctance to review tracts also stemmed from Macaulay's judgment that many tracts were third-rate literature. From a pragmatic point of view, literary merit was necessary if tracts were to lure "the listless" to virtue. However, establishing such criteria was a significant step, implying the inadequacy of exclusively moral criticism and foreshadowing the dissociation of literature and religion. In June 1806, the *Observer* took the leap. In criticizing *The Cottage Library of Christian Knowledge; a New Series of Religious Tracts*, the journal measured a collection of tracts by a literary standard for the first time. In the past too many tracts, in particular those published by the Religious Tract Society, the *Observer* wrote, had been "too much like sermons" and "not sufficiently popular and attractive to engage the attention of the persons for whose benefit they were principally intended." "To obviate this objection," the Society now published *The Cottage*. Unfortunately, however, *The Cottage* was poor literature. Not only was it sometimes vulgar, but it often disregarded "the established rules of good writing" and showed "a want of meaning." "Any clumsy limner may load his canvas with light," the journal declared, but "it is the judicious disposition of light and shade which gives effect to the picture." Instead of writing new tracts, the Religious Tract Society (the *Observer* advised) would do better to circulate the *Cheap Repository Tracts* which were "monuments of that union of genius and piety, of which there have been too few examples in the world" (V, 372–375).

Although modified by literary considerations, the moral

criterion remained the *Observer's* primary yardstick. In its next major literary critique, a review of Bowdler's *The Family Shakespeare* in May 1808, standards were exclusively ethical. Bowdler's book provided the *Observer* with an opportunity to discuss dangers of fiction. After granting that Fielding, Smollett, and Richardson were among "our standard classics," the *Observer* argued that *Tom Jones, Clarissa,* and *Roderick Random* were "unfit for general perusal." Even *Don Quixote* was "inadmissible into the domestic library," and Mrs. Radcliffe's heroes and heroines were "not formed after the model laid down in the New Testament" (VII, 332–333).

More importantly, the novel's appeal to the imagination harmed the youth who had not formed good habits and who longed "to disengage himself from his aurelia state, and flutter airily in the beams of what he" was "enjoined to call sensibility" (327). Although the *Observer* did not completely proscribe the imagination, it called poetry, romance, and drama "the auxiliaries of vice" and urged readers to exercise their imaginations in the cause of religion, writing: "In our opinion, every intellectual power finds its place in religion. The prophetic imagery of the Old Testament, and the parables of the New, may be regarded as properly the offspring of the inventive faculty. But the ornamental and symbolic language of the Scripture is throughout employed in urging the human mind to exert its highest powers on subjects of eternal importance" (334).

The Bowdler review was an extreme of literature for Christianity's sake, but as such it underlined the journal's vacillating attitude toward the novel. Moreover, the *Observer's* struggle with the novel was but a microcosm of the Claphams' struggle to be both evangelical Anglicans and respected Tories. Consistency was difficult. In the Preface to the ninth volume (1810), the *Observer* stated: "It is not easy, in a feverish state of society, to preserve one's-self from occasional heat. It is not easy to manage the gas and ballast of the machine, when assailed by the blasts of invective, or tossed in the storms of controversy" (iii). Although this statement was directed at politics, it was also applicable to literary matters.

Aware of the extreme position of the Bowdler review, the *Observer* printed a biting rebuttal by Bowdler's nephew, writing anonymously as Philalethes. Defending the imagination as "one of the most powerful causes of civilization." Philalethes argued that if the principles of the Bowdler review were "generally embraced by the readers of the *Christian Observer,* they would probably in the next age be reduced to a sect of low bigots, and in the following be divided between weak enthusiasts and furious fanatics" (VII, 391–392).

Accusing the journal of literary jingoism, Philalethes declared, "Of all things in the world a terrorist is the most troublesome. He sighs and grumbles till other melancholy souls catch the infection; and then, as numbers give confidence, the prophesyings begin. All who are silly, ignorant, timid, or discontented, become possessed. Old bachelors, tyrannical husbands, country gentlemen of decayed fortunes with their ancient housekeepers, the second rates of a party, doctors of physic who have no patients, citizens retired to

Finchley, with an hundred more, join in the clamour, and alarm spreads in every direction" (392).

Philalethes' points were well taken. His combination of ridicule and argument balanced the Bowdler review. Aware of its weak ground, the *Observer* felt obliged to answer, saying that they did not mean to proscribe all works of the imagination which did not find a place in the Bible, but only to plead that some works counteracted "the dream of Christianity." If it could be shown that novels convinced selfish people to do good deeds, the *Observer* wrote, "their tendency to give an undue elevation to persons of a romantic turn might perhaps be forgiven. But we fear . . . their operation is not so much to raise the mind to nobler purposes, as to produce a disinclination to regular industry, and to quicken the appetite for low and vicious pursuits" (VII, 395).

In this state of suspended critical animation, the matter of the novel rested unresolved until February 1809, when the *Observer* reviewed Hannah More's *Coelebs in Search of a Wife*. Throughout the first decade of the century, Hannah More had become progressively disturbed by the number of circulating libraries. Higher book prices and increased taxation for the Napoleonic Wars coincided with the rapid growth of British literacy, with the result that there was a large number of readers who could not afford to buy many books. To fulfill the demand for inexpensive reading, circulating libraries multiplied. Believing that the "refuse of the circulating-library" was pitched at the lowest moral denominator, Hannah More thought the libraries' indiscriminant lists now threatened British morality, much as seditious writings had threatened the Constitution in the 1790's. As she had with the *Cheap Repository,* so Hannah More now rose to the occasion, writing *Coelebs* as a paradigm of what the novel could and should be. Hopefully *Coelebs* would establish the religious novel as a staple of the circulating library and like the *Tracts* "form the moral sentiments and judgments of the young."[11]

Disguised as autobiography, *Coelebs* was a relentlessly didactic novel, or as Sydney Smith called it a "dramatic sermon." Describing an evangelical young man's search for an ideal wife, the novel was constructed around a series of parable-like situations illustrating the material and spiritual benefits that accrued to true Christians. Conversely, irreligion was showed to have disastrous consequences. Each situation had its accompanying sermon, like a coda, so that sermon by sermon the novel exposed the flaws of fashionable life. Education, poetry, the opera, and Sunday Schools were among the multitude of things discussed. With the exception of the "religious" Stanleys, the characters were the stock dramatis personae of fashionable novels. Instead of using them to bring vicarious pleasure to readers by describing the high life above the stairs, however, Mrs. More used her characters as pawns in theological discussions. With the flaws of their various ways of life carefully exposed, one by one they fell before Mrs. More's king, the ideal Mr. Stanley.[12]

Although he did not know Hannah More wrote *Coelebs* (the book was published anonymously), Macaulay was overwhelmed by the novel and thought it set a standard for which

11. *Eclectic Review,* 1 (1805), "Prospectus," 2. Roberts, *Memoirs,* III, 272–273, 291.
12. *Edinburgh Review,* 14 (1809), 145–146.

all novels should aim.[13] Aware that the word "novel" waved a red flag before some readers, Macaulay did not call *Coelebs* a novel; rather, he stressed the book's difference from the ordinary novel. According to Macaulay, *Coelebs* resembled a string of parables in which the author was concerned not so much with "an interesting fable," but with communicating "a variety of religious, moral, and economical truths, in an easy and agreeable manner" (VIII, 109). If *Coelebs* partook "slightly of the character and peculiarities" of the novel, this broadened the book's appeal (110). Writing that the *"first, great* object" of the author was to instruct, Macaulay lectured other novelists on technique, with such advice as: "We have often wondered that novel-writers, careless as they are of every thing but how they may surprise or please, should never have suspected that the infusion of religious principles and feelings into the character of a heroine would add greatly to the interest of the piece" (115, 118–119).

Of the story itself, Macaulay wrote that it had the "one prime excellence" of being "perfectly in nature" (111). Romance did not undermine the book's lessons as it did in Mrs. Radcliffe's novels, where, for example, "the lurid flames" of her imagination kindled all about them (115). Instead of stimulating the imagination, Mrs. More's characters were signposts pointing the way to heaven. Mr. Stanley was,

13. The review's extravagant praise notwithstanding, Mrs. More was displeased by several minor criticisms. She was particularly irritated by Macaulay's good-humored criticism of the book's title. "A squire of Westmoreland," he wrote, "may go *in search* of grouse or woodcocks; but, to beat about thus for a wife, is not altogether so well imagined. Girls may be thought fair game; yet they are not quite on a level with red-legged partridges" (120).

Macaulay wrote, "a portrait which it required something more than genius, enriched by observation, to execute; for as Milton declares that no one can be a poet who it not himself the epitome of a good poem, so we may venture to say, that he who could sketch this exalted character must have felt in his own bosom the power of holiness—that he is himself, in some measure, the great sublime he teaches" (112).

The ideal, generic heroine who would not cause schoolboys to flutter about in their aurelia state, Lucilla gave Macaulay more difficulty. Nevertheless, he made her weakness appear her strength, writing: "Angelic as Lucilla's character really is, we are not without fears that the men will think it insipid. There is no helping this; very good people are apt to seem insipid. Religion is such a neutralizer of the character, that, unless pious women are loved for their piety, they must often be content to be passed by altogether . . . We have sometimes thought that persons of eminent holiness are like pellucid bodies, which philosophers tell us contain more matter than opaque ones; but every part being justly distributed, the light passes freely through, nothing detains the eye, and they are as if they were not" (113).

The whole review was cut from this panegyrical cloth and was remarkable for a journal formerly hostile to the novel. To Macaulay the strain of leaning on novelistic techniques while condemning novels out of hand must have been burdensome. Swept away by his approval of *Coelebs* and sense of relief at resolving the *Observer's* critical inconsistency toward the novel, Macaulay ended his critique with a prayer. "May the Father of all Goodness," he wrote, "bless this work to his glory, in the advancement of piety and happiness. To

Him, doubtless, it is an acceptable sacrifice; and what are the applauses, even of the wise and good, compared with his favour, 'in whose presence is life, and at whose right hand are pleasures fore ever more?' " (121)

The *Christian Observer* had crossed a critical Rubicon. In December in review of Maria Edgeworth's *Tales of Fashionable Life*, Volumes I–III, Macaulay corrected the embarrassing effusiveness of the *Coelebs* review and in doing so put the *Observer's* critical shift from enmity to toleration of and even appreciation of the novel on a firmer basis. The review began by justifying the *Observer's* examination of Maria Edgeworth's works, which religious journals had resoundingly condemned for failing to teach that "in every system of Education religion should be the *corner stone.*"[14] To the reader who was surprised at finding the *Observer* "entering upon this new department of literature, and wandering so far from the precincts of the sanctuary," the journal declared, "every novel by an author of reputation is an object of solicitude to the guardians of the public morals" (VIII, 781).

After this major departure from past practice, the *Observer* considered the thorny problem of the imagination. Philalethes' common sense carried the day as the journal championed a reasonable use of the imagination, writing, "If the danger of all writings of imagination or sentiment be objected to us; and if it be affirmed, that to criticise is to tolerate them; we answer, that it forms no part of our creed that *all* such works should be transferred from the shelves to the fire of the library. If we think them mischievous to the

14. *Guardian of Education*, 1 (1802), 496.

young, to the weaker sex, to the frivolous, and to the sanguine; we yet conceive that minds of a solid texture, and of established principles, may occasionally read them, if not with benefit, at least without injury. The vice of the present age is not, let it be remembered, too much romance, but too much coldness and selfishness. We are not in danger of becoming a nation of crusaders, but of merchants. Now a suitable remedy for this, under the regulation of Christian principles, is an infusion of sentiment into the general system" (781).

Compared to this critical declaration, analysis of the *Tales* was secondary. Because of a festering quarrel with the *Edinburgh Review* which championed Maria Edgeworth, and because of the absence of evangelical doctrine, the *Observer* dealt harshly with the *Tales*. "Works like those of Miss Edgeworth's," the journal stated, "are to be considered as bold and (must we say it?) impious experiments whether we can do without religion: and it is at our peril that we acquiesce in them, till it can be demonstrated that we have no souls" (790).

Over the next three years the *Christian Observer* did not advance its critical theories. Tacitly admitting that the novel could be used for good, the *Observer* probed deeper into the moral flaw of what they now called "the Edgeworth school." In reviews of Volumes IV–VI of the *Tales of Fashionable Life* and of Mary Leadbeater's *Cottage Dialogues,* for which Maria Edgeworth had written an enthusiastic preface, the *Observer* repeatedly preached the dangers of a fictional world without religion. Throughout these years, the *Observer* compared Hannah More's morality with that of the Edgeworth

School. Despite her desire to help the poor, Mrs. Leadbeater's *Cottage Dialogues,* for example, were held to be inferior to the *Cheap Repository Tracts* in which were found "lessons of the most momentous import skillfully blended with familiar sketches of humble life and manners." "They [the *Tracts*] insinuate knowledge without appearing to teach," the *Observer* wrote, "and while no branch even of domestic economy and housewifery, however minute, is excluded from the moral delineations which they exhibit, they are uniformly and successfully directed to far higher objects" (X, 238–239).

In December 1812 the novel passed another milestone on the way to critical respectability as the *Observer* established Aristotelian categories for the best novels. Since the word *novel* evoked an unfavorable response, the journal's categories were for "works of fiction." Although these included poetry and nonfictional prose, primary emphasis was on the novel. Out of hand the *Observer* dismissed the third category in which moral didacticism was incidental to the narrative. The second category included works containing an "evident moral throughout" but which were "worked up in a manner to please the imagination or touch the heart, independently of that moral." Evidently the *Observer's* opinion of Maria Edgeworth had mellowed, because she was included in this category along with "almost all the noblest efforts of poetry" (XI, 782–783).

In contrast to this second class, which instructed by pleasing, was the first, which pleased by instructing. These were works written solely to instruct and which derived their interest from the lesson conveyed. Not only did this class include Plato's *Republic*, More's *Utopia*, and Bunyan's *Pilgrim's Progress*, but also biblical allegories and parables, which the *Observer* called "the most perfect instances on record of the use of fiction disjoined from all its bad properties." Even sentiment was praised: "the allegory of the 'Prodigal Son,' whilst it is simply and solely intended to illustrate and encourage the great act of genuine repentance, presents a series of the most affecting and heart-touching incidents to the imagination which are to be found in all the annals of sentiment" (782).

With the story of the Prodigal Son now acknowledged as the archetypical sentimental tale appealing to the imagination, the imagination, or rather the *Observer's* attitude toward it, had changed considerably. After stating that they endeavored only "to throw before our readers some rough material for making their own decision on any work of invention," the *Observer* declared as a sop to hard-bitten opponents of the novel that it would not be suitable to appear too conversant with the form. "Wading through an infinity of pernicious trash, for the sake of arriving at a single honest, well-meant, and well-executed effort at instruction, in the garb of interesting and popular fiction," would, the *Observer* wrote, set a "dangerous example" (785).

Behind these harsh words, though, lay the important admission that some novels belonged in the first two categories. And if Maria Edgeworth's works were in the second class, at least one novel, *Coelebs*, belonged with the Prodigal Son. In the pages of the *Christian Observer* the novel had won its major battle for respectability and broken through crucial moral barriers. Although skirmishes over the imagination and the novel would still flare up periodically, fervor and conviction had gone out of the controversy.

In 1816 a tired Zachary Macaulay turned the editorship of the *Observer* over to Samuel Wilks. Lacking Macaulay's critical sense and broad view, Wilks had second thoughts about the novel. And in 1822, in reviewing Scott's *The Pirate*, the *Observer* attacked the novel, repeating the threadbare arguments against the imagination and urging Scott to turn his talents to glorifying God and benefiting his fellow man.

Despite Wilks's moral enthusiasm, the review was dated and carried little weight. In fact, the game was given away on the second page. "Go where you will," the reviewer admitted, "a Waverley Novel peeps forth: you will find it on the breakfast table, and under the pillow; concealed in the desk of the clerk, and the till of shopman; in the sleeve of the gownsman, and the pocket of the squire; on the barouchebox, and in the sword-case; by day-light, by lamp-light, by moon-light, by rush-light; aye, even among the Creek Indians has been seen a volume of these far-famed tales beguiling the tedious hours of the daughter of an Alabama planter, as she sat down with her coffee-pot by the evening fireside in the recesses of an American forest" (XXII, 158). The *Observer's* earlier approval of the genre coincided with popular moral opinion. In the 1820's and '30's, a few people would still protest against the novel, but these were a distinct minority.

Chapter 3
Coelebs in Search of a Wife, and *Waverley*

In discussing *The Pirate,* the *Observer* stated that Scott's novels had been "the means of breaking down the barrier which had been hitherto maintained between the habits of *bona fide* Christians, and the habits of worldly society." This view of Scott as popularizer of the novel has become a saw of historical criticism. In *Novels of the Eighteen-Forties,* for example, Kathleen Tillotson maintained that Scott, more than any other author, was responsible for the novel's becoming respectable reading in the nineteenth century. Breaching moral opposition to the genre, Scott prepared the way for Dickens, and by midcentury the novel was the dominant literary form. Certainly the sale of Scott's novels support Professor Tillotson's historical view. *Waverley* (1814), for example, sold 6,000 copies in six months; *Rob Roy* (1818), 10,000 in a fortnight. Nevertheless this history of the novel's popularity overlooks the preparatory importance of religious tracts and the phenomenal success enjoyed by Hannah More's *Coelebs.* The first nineteenth century novel to be acclaimed by "religious readers," *Coelebs* convinced many doubters, like Macaulay, that the novel could become a handmaiden to Christianity. As a result, the public was prepared for Scott, whose concerns, if not particularly theological, were safely moral.[1]

Today *Coelebs* reads like a creaky period piece. As a boy Coelebs had become "enamoured" of "Milton's Eve"; and later whenever his fancy lightly turned to thoughts of "conjugal happiness," his mind "involuntarily adverted to the graces of that finished picture." Inheriting a considerable estate in one of the northern counties after the death of his father, Coelebs decided to marry. After judging the local girls unfinished rather than finished, at "not quite four and twenty," he set out for fashionable London and the home of his father's friends Sir John and Lady Belfield on Cavendish Square. Well-bred, but alas too latitudinarian, the Belfields had a wide acquaintance. Through them Coelebs met the Ranbys, Lady Bab Lawless, Mrs. Fentham, and Lady Melbury. Although intellectually and socially a mixed lot, all Coelebs' new acquaintances lacked true Christianity. Mrs. Fentham, for example, worshipped the world, not God, while Mrs. Ranby believed religion a matter of instantaneous conversion. Consequently she paid little attention to good deeds, and following her example, her three daughters idled their days away waiting for divine guidance. In contrast to these characters was the unfashionable family of Mr. Stanley whom Coelebs visited after the Belfields. His father's closest friend, Mr. Stanley was "a genuine bible Christian." At Stanley Grove in Hampshire, Coelebs not only found his Eve, Mr. Stanley's oldest daughter Lucilla, who adorned "every virtue with every grace," but also heard soul-stirring discussions of right Christian behavior. Abuses of the novel,

1. *Christian Observer,* 22 (1822), 158. Tillotson, pp. 15–16.

poetry, and children's books, dangers of superstition, errors of dress, true charity, education of children, and the place of women were but a few of the many subjects on which Mr. Stanley explained the Christian's position. Moreover, Mr. Stanley's general "sermons" were given particular emphasis by the flaws of neighbors and old friends who visited him— with the result that by the end of the novel, the reader and Coelebs had heard more than a score of sermons and had met as many characters whose misfortunes resulted from their lack of or flawed faiths. Not even Coelebs' successful courtship and the happy discovery that long years before, his father and Mr. Stanley had planned for him and Lucilla to marry can help us understand the excitement that boiled at the book's publication. According to James Stephen, speculation over the mysterious author stirred up as much private gossip as Junius' *Letters* or Chatterton's *Poems* stirred up public controversy. A run-away best seller, "all the world" was "mad to read it." Eleven editions appeared in nine months, and it was rumored that the book was printed simultaneously at three different locations.[2]

In the first quarter of the nineteenth century, no novel was so widely reviewed as *Coelebs*. Most reviews were enthusiastic. The stodgy *British Critic* had "not read a work which" combined "the *utile cum dulci* more completely than Coelebs." Writing that every part of *Coelebs* tended "to good,"

2. Roberts. *Memoirs*, III, 289. Hannah More, *Coelebs in Search of a Wife, Comprehending Observations on Domestic Habits and Manners, Religion and Morals* (London, 1809), I, 1, 142, 200. By 1818 fifteen "large" editions of *Coelebs* had appeared. By the time of Mrs. More's death in 1833, some 30,000 copies of the novel had been sold in the United States. *London Review*, 1 (1809), 425.

journals recommended "its perusal to every virtuous family in the British Empire." After saying that some of the characters were "rather dull," the *Scots Magazine* waxed rhapsodically metaphorical, declaring: "But in Coelebs, as in Achilles, there is but a heel that is vulnerable; and after our severest operation, he looks even better than before. Winnow this book as we please, there still remains a full and nutritious grain behind. Its feathers may be plucked; but it only tends the better to lay bare a plump and full-fed body, which when scientifically served up, will, we promise, afford as savoury, and satisfying a repast, as ever touched the table, or pleased the palate of an intellectual epicure." Even more remarkable was the forty-three line tribute in the *Poetical Magazine*. According to the anonymous versifier, "Long had a false but specious taste prevail'd / Thro' which our youths were fatally assail'd." The "floating novels of the day" had corrupted not only the young virgin, the servant wench, the 'prentic'd lad, and student for the bench, but also the prelate and the fair who glittered at the court. Dipping their pens in "error's wand'ring stream," previous novelists had written for the body and forgotten the soul. In contrast *Coelebs* formed "the grand design" of speaking of "truths divine" and explaining "Salvation's great and glorious plan."[3]

The few journals that condemned *Coelebs* did so primarily on the grounds of its religiosity. For the most part, these journals unfairly identified Mrs. More's Anglican evangel-

3. *British Critic,* 33 (1809), 490. *Literary Panorama,* 6 (1809), 268. *Satirist,* 4 (1809), 389. *Scots Magazine,* 71 (1809), 518, 524. *Poetical Magazine,* 1 (1809), 307–308.

icalism with aeolian methodism. One periodical asserted that the sentiments taught by *Coelebs* were "those of methodism, with all its vile cant and all its holy perversion." Combining personal vituperation with theological criticism, another journal wrote that although Coelebs tried to reverse the stratagem of Achilles by disguising himself in the dress of a young man of twenty-five, his "eagerness to grasp the quill of religious controversy" betrayed the illusion and sent "him forth to the holy wars in the shape of an old lady of seventy." The *London Review* said that *Coelebs* was a novel for "conventiclers, and suckling none but the babes of grace with the pure milk of divine love." In the midst of a whitehot quarrel with the Claphams, Sydney Smith flayed *Coelebs* in the *Edinburgh Review*. After calling the main character a dolt and saying that Lucilla was totally uninteresting, Smith apologized sarcastically, writing that if Mrs. More had not belonged to a trumpery gospel faction and had not degraded the human understanding to the trash and folly of methodism, she would have been one of the most valuable writers of the day.[4]

The bite in these unfavorable reviews indirectly testified to *Coelebs'* popularity and underlined the reason for the novel's sensational sales. Most readers and journals thought this combination of religion and the novel constituted a new literary genre. The *Monthly Magazine* and the *Scots Magazine* were uneasy with "the plan of mixing up religion" with the novel. The *London Review* said that *Coelebs* should

4. *Universal Magazine*, 11 (1809), 517. *Walker's Hibernian Magazine* (1809), 332. *London Review*, 1 (1809), 426. *Edinburgh Review*, 14 (1809), 146, 151.

have been called "SERIOUS DIALOGUES ON FAITH AND GOOD WORKS," while the *Critical Review* characterized *Coelebs* as "not so much a regular story as a series of conversations, in which the object of the author is to recommend his own theological opinions." Unsure of what it was, the *Monthly Review* weakly called it "something" which assumed "the form of a novel." In contrast, the *European Magazine*, publishing its review late in 1809, after most reviews had already appeared, printed a long apologia in which they proved that "conveying instruction through the medium of a tale" had a long and respectable past. Upon Bunyan's respectable foundation, the *European Magazine* wrote, Defoe erected his *"religious superstructure."* Unfortunately, Richardson, more artificial than Defoe, had entangled "his story with all the intricacies of art." In contrast *Coelebs* returned to the moral fountainhead and avoided "the vagaries of romantic wildness."[5]

In a harsh but perceptive review, the *Universal Magazine* said that *Coelebs's* "extraordinary sale" could be "accounted for upon the same principles as that of the *Evangelical Magazine*, or any antinomian tract." The novel found "purchasers among those the majority of whom would discard with pious indignation a Shakespeare or a Milton from their shelves." The *Universal Magazine* wrongly discounted the "fashionable world," which also read *Coelebs* eagerly, but the journal was right in believing that it was the first novel thought by nineteenth century religious readers to be mor-

5. *Monthly Magazine,* 27 (1809), 663. *Scots Magazine,* 71 (1809), 438. *London Review,* 1 (1809), 425. *Critical Review,* 16 (1809), 261. *Monthly Review,* 58 (1809), 128. *European Magazine,* 56 (1809), 198.

ally respectable. The *Evangelical Magazine* wrote in its critique: "It was mentioned in one of our recent Numbers, that wherever the Poison-tree grows, its antidote grows very near it. This is a gracious disposition of Providence; and we are happy to find that something similar obtains in the literary world. The groves of Literature have, within the last 50 years, been poisoned with infidel and licentious novels and romances; but in this and a few other similar works, we behold the antidote to such dangerous publications. Here, with at least equal interest and entertainment, the reader will find the wisest maxims of life and conduct, and even the holy principles of religion."[6]

James Stephen urged Hannah More to write another novel, saying he hoped *Coelebs* would "not always be left like a pilgrim in an African forest, to be followed and surrounded by monkey-imitators, without a companion from the same rational stock to support him in his pious enterprise." Stephen was disappointed; Mrs. More did not write another novel, but others did, and *Nubilia in Search of a Husband, Celia in Search of a Husband,* and *Coelebs Married* were soon swinging by their tails through presses.[7]

Despite the lack of proper companions for *Coelebs,* however, Mrs. More's pious enterprise was continued. Her book had shown suspicious readers that the land of fiction, even if it did not flow with milk and honey, could at least provide healthy, moral entertainment. If one were careful to avoid the Poison-trees, one just might be able to discover a fictional

6. *Universal Magazine,* 11 (1809), 523. *Evangelical Magazine,* 17 (1809), 289.

7. Roberts, *Memoirs,* III, 308.

lily of the valley or rose of Sharon in the groves of literature. As a result Andrew Reed was able to find a large audience for *No Fiction*, and John Cunningham's *The Velvet Cushion* became the subject of much controversy in religious journals. More importantly, Walter Scott wrote *Waverley*, which if it did not embody Mrs. More's particular faith was at least consciously moral and convinced readers, in Trollope's words, of Scott's "conviction of his duty as a teacher."

Factors apart from the book's rigorously correct morality and the fact that *Coelebs* had smoothed the way contributed to the success of *Waverley*. As an historical novel, *Waverley* made a doubly strong appeal to religious readers. Those believing that history and biography were higher forms of literature than the novel applauded the book's historicism. Likewise the fears of those who thought novels threatened the imagination were assuaged by the historical basis of the story and characters. According to the *British Critic*, *Waverley* was so exceptional that it should not be considered "in the light of a common novel," whose fate it was "to be devoured with rapidity for the day, and to be afterwards forgotten for ever." For the *Critic*, *Waverley* was an historical parable whose account of the "bloody days" of 1745 should "by an early and awful warning inspire the nation with a jealous vigilance against the very first symptoms of their recurrence." Although "the frame" of *Waverley* was fiction, the *Monthly Review* saw no danger to readers' imaginations, writing that the narrative was "as correct, minute, and spirited a copy of nature as ever came from the hands of an artist." This fidelity to nature was an important ingredient in Scott's success. Throughout his career, critics praised him for being "less of a dealer in *heroes* than most novel-writers," for painting "portraits from real life," and for creating characters which delighted "lovers of genuine nature."[8] In *Waverley* Scott got double value from his history. In "fictionalizing" the bloody days of 1745, Scott had merely followed the lead of religious journals, which had been writing "better" history and biography for years. In 1814 in his *History of Fiction,* John Dunlop praised the morality of this technique. "Real history," Dunlop wrote, did not give the "success of things according to the deserts of vice and virtue." In contrast fiction was always able to reward virtue and to teach "morality and nobleness of soul." Taking an overview of Scott's first three novels, the *Critical Review* and the *Augustan Review* agreed with Dunlop, with the former calling Scott's novels "fictitious realities" and the latter saying they were "*philosophical histories,* which delineate in a way much more enchanting than history, the habits, the manners, the workings of the human mind."[9]

In discussing Dunlop's *History,* the *British Critic* wrote that "no country or age" had cultivated the novel "with so much attention to its moral effect" as had Britain. Reflecting this ethical tradition, *Waverley* appealed to a wide spectrum of moralists. Even the high church *Anti-Jacobin* praised the book handsomely. To their mind, Scott revived those days "when writers of genius, information, and talents" wrote

8. *British Critic,* 2 (1814), 190, 204. *Monthly Review,* 75 (1814), 275; 82 (1817), 39. *British Lady's Magazine,* 1 (1815), 356. *European Magazine,* 70 (1816), 249.

9. John Dunlop, *The History of Fiction* (London, 1814), I, viii. *Critical Review,* 3 (1816), 487. *Augustan Review,* 3 (1816), 155.

novels. Since the French Revolution, the *Anti-Jacobin* wrote, London presses had published "shoals of composition" which exhibited "the national character in a contemptible point of view" and which had "no small effect in relaxing the vigour of moral principles in the younger part of the present generation."[10]

The first chapter of *Waverley* was a critical essay in which Scott assured potential readers that his morality was correct and in which he methodically dissociated himself from other novelists by explaining why he chose *Waverley: or 'Tis Sixty Years Since* as a title. In contrast to the "chivalrous epithets" of Howard or Mordaunt and the "sentimental sounds" of Belmour or Belgrave, Waverley, he wrote, was "an uncontaminated name, bearing with its sound little of good or evil, excepting what the reader shall be hereafter pleased to affix to it" (I, 4). At a stroke he had declared his disapproval of Minerva Press books: "the soft, senseless, and effeminate romances" which critics thought perverted "the morals and the taste of the rising generation."[11]

Next Scott separated himself from the gothic novel and its dangers to the imagination, explaining that he had not subtitled *Waverley* "a Tale of Other Days" because readers would have "anticipated a castle scarce less than that of Udolpho" (I, 5). Throughout the book Scott implicitly criticized the gothic novel by emphasizing the difference between reality and sentiment. Travelling to Tully-Veolan, for exam-

10. *British Critic*, 2 (1814), 168. *Anti-Jacobin*, 47 (1814), 217.
11. Walter Scott, *Waverley: or 'Tis Sixty Years Since* (Edinburgh, 1814). The parentheses in the text refer to volume and page. *Scots Magazine*, 71 (1809), 437.

ple, Waverley dreamed that the Bradwardines' home resembled a gothic castle. Instead of passing through "wild and romantic" vales, however, he rode through the village of Tully-Veolan with dogs barking at his horse's heels. Instead of seeing "the Apennines in their darkest horrors," he saw peasants' huts bordered by stacks of turf and family dung-heaps. In contrast to a "gloomy and sublime object" standing the "sovereign of the scene" and frowning "defiance on all," he found the Bradwardines' manor house hidden by trees and surrounded by gardens. Cosmo Bradwardine, himself, was no Montoni but a delightful eccentric. Scott's audience applauded this criticism, and the *Monthy Review* wrote enthusiastically that *Waverley* had little of the ordinary attractions of the novel to recommend it. Readers would find, the journal said, that the book was "strictly an historical romance" and was different from titles such as *Emmeline* and *Castel Gandolpho*.[12]

In the last decade of the eighteenth century and the first of the nineteenth, the German gothic novel had become a popular commodity in circulating libraries. For Hannah More such novels were obviously written by "modern apostles of infidelity and immorality." The *Anti-Jacobin* held that novels were responsible for Germany's jacobinical morality. To warn Britons of the dangers of all things German, they printed a description of "a pitiful Englishman completely Germanized, who used seriously to maintain that England had no cause to boast of liberty, seeing the marriage chains were so difficult to be broken, whereas in Germany

12. Anne Radcliffe, *The Mysteries of Udolpho* (London, 1966), pp. 226–227. *Monthly Review*, 75 (1814), 279–280.

nothing is more easy than to get rid of one's wife, and both get married again, or pursue their inclinations without any interruption of their friendship." Aware of such criticisms, Scott assured readers he would never subtitle a book "a Romance from the German." It went without saying, though he said it, that he would not call a novel a "Sentimental Tale" (I, 5–6).[13]

Making *Waverley* even more attractive to religious readers, Scott criticized novels of "the fashionable world" (I, 6), thereby dissociating himself from Maria Edgeworth's questionable morality. The *Anti-Jacobin* picked this up and favorably compared him to her, writing that they could not tell whether Mrs. Edgeworth's novels were written by a pagan or by a Christian.[14]

At the conclusion of the first chapter, Scott evoked the respectable shadow of Dr. Johnson, writing that *Waverley* described those passions common to men in all stages of society and which had "alike agitated the human heart, whether it throbbed under the steel corselet of the fifteenth century, the brocaded coat of the eighteenth, or the blue frock and white dimity waistcoat of the present day" (I, 10). Similarly, Johnson thought man's nature remained constant through the ages. Although deformities appeared in individuals, Johnson believed artists should not copy them, but instead see beyond the surface and the particular to the general and the ideal. Consequently artists had not only a moral but an artistic duty to better their fellow men by depicting the ideal. Carried to the extreme, this led to the novel's being

13. More, *Strictures*, I, 39. *Anti-Jacobin*, 5 (1800), 579.
14. *Anti-Jacobin*, 47 (1814), 217.

a parable filled with generic characters—just the sort of thing written by Hannah More and Rowland Hill.[15]

Although Scott did not go so far as Hill or More, his first chapter prepared readers for, if not an extended parable, at least a highly moral novel. The second chapter neglected moral concerns in order to give a synopsis of the Waverley family history. However, aimed directly at religious readers, the third chapter examined education, a topic frequently discussed in religious journals. A lesson in how not to educate a child, Edward Waverley's education was so central to the didacticism of the narrative that the *British Critic* expostulated "Let those who are engaged in forming the minds of the youth of this country not disdain to receive a hint even from the trifling pages of a novel."[16]

Edward Waverley had not received a rigorous education. More importantly, no one had disciplined his reading so that he "drove through the sea of books, like a vessel without a pilot or a rudder" (I, 37). Consequently, he became a "youthful visionary . . . unfit for serious and sober study" (I, 42–43). "His imagination, the predominant faculty of his mind" was filled "with visions as brilliant and as fading as those of an evening sky" (I, 45, 53). To religious readers, Waverley was, of course, a stock character: the promising youth led astray by sensibility. As he went through life substituting sentiment for morality and good sense, he would sink lower until he eventually died or was reformed by an apocalyptic experience.

Step by step Scott chronicled the errors resulting from the

15. See *Rambler 4*.
16. *British Critic*, 2 (1814), 209.

youth's education. Waverley's inflamed imagination led him to the outlaw Donald Bean Lean. Moreover, when compared to those of Rose Bradwardine, Flora Mac-Ivor's attractions were insubstantial; but she was, in Scott's words, "precisely the character to fascinate a youth of romantic imagination" (II, 6). Unable to distinguish virtue from fanaticism, Waverley proposed to Flora. So that readers would not miss the point, Fergus asked Waverley if he were serious or just in "the land of romance and fiction" (II, 61). Flora herself told Waverley that he proposed only because she was an unusual woman "in a sequestered and romantic situation" (II, 72). As Waverley got into deeper trouble with the rebels, Scott frequently discussed the youth's romantic imagination, with the result that no reader could fail to see that a faulty education was at the root of the boy's difficulties.

The parable of the Prodigal Son supplied the narrative framework for many tracts and for numerous biographies in religious journals. Aware of his audience, Scott used the parable as the dramatic skeleton of *Waverley*, as well as *Guy Mannering* and, to a lesser extent, *The Antiquary*. Like the Prodigal Son, Waverley metaphorically squandered his birthright, with the result that awareness was thrust upon him, not by eating husks, but by the death of his servant Houghton. Finding Houghton mortally wounded and learning from him that the men from Waverley-Honour had been led astray by Donald Bean Lean, Waverley suddenly realized that in indulging his imagination he had neglected his duty to his fellow man. Houghton's cry "Ah squire, why did you leave us?" rang, Scott wrote, like a bell in Waverley's ears.

At Houghton's death, Waverley saw the flaw in his own nature and subsequently confessed his errors in a dramatic soliloquy that had the same rhythm and import as the General Confession (II, 343).

After his confession, Waverley's biography resembled that of the repentant sinner. Slowly his understanding of himself and his world increased. In describing the battle of Preston Pans, Scott provided religious readers with a narrative key to the novel's moral core. On the field, Waverley found Colonel Gardiner, a father figure and the British officer from whose forces Waverley had deserted. Colonel James Gardiner was an actual historic character. Nicknamed *"The Happy Rake,"* Gardiner lived riotously until one evening after returning home from an assignation with a married woman, he picked up Thomas Watson's *The Christian Soldier, or Heaven Taken by Storm.* While Gardiner read for diversion, a blaze of light fell on the book. Above him appeared "a visible Representation of the *Lord Jesus Christ* upon the Cross, surrounded on all Sides with a Glory." A voice, or "something equivalent to a Voice" said "Oh Sinner, did I suffer this for thee, and are these the Returns?"[17]

Gardiner's days of dueling and nights of roving ended shortly thereafter. And although his friends thought him *"stark mad,"* he became *"the Christian Hero."* After Gardiner was killed at Preston Pans, Phillip Doddridge enshrined him in a moral biography. The biography became extremely popular, and Gardiner became the inspirational

17. Philip Doddridge, *Some Remarkable Passages in the Life of the Hon. Colonel James Gardiner* (London, 1747), pp. 21, 30–32, 61, 190.

type of the repentant sinner, so much so that the Religious Tract Society issued an edition of the biography as their seventeenth tract.

In Scott's novel, while Gardiner lay dying, he gazed reproachfully at Waverley. As Doddridge's biography of the reformed sinner had showed the path of reformation to its readers, so Gardiner's look showed Waverley where his duty lay. Shortly after the officer's death, Waverley stopped brooding over his past sins and, shouldering his burden, began to show concern for others. When he assumed responsibility for Colonel Talbot, his character improved rapidly so that by the end of the novel the fatted calf was metaphorically slaughtered and Waverley pardoned for his sins.

In 1787 the *Arminian Magazine* wrote that the Christian parable was an "extended similitude, in which objects of a moral or spiritual nature" were "represented by images or examples drawn from things sensible, and from the occurrences of life." Because of their narrative form, the journal wrote, parables made "a more shining and lasting impression on the mind."[18] As a parable, *Waverley* made a lasting impression upon religious readers. Convinced he had discovered a successful narrative formula, Scott repeated it in *Guy Mannering*. Although the narrative of *Guy Mannering* differed from that of *Waverley*, many thematic concerns were similar. In the history of the heir of Ellangowan, Scott produced a variant of the prodigal son story. Moreover, Julia Mannering, her father, and her mother all suffered from "luxuriant imaginations" as Scott again attacked the novel of sensibil-

18. *Arminian Magazine*, 10 (1787), 155, 209.

ity. Parodying sensibility, Julia Mannering's letters illustrated the bad effects of reading gothic tales and fashionable
novels. To drive home his criticism of sensibility, Scott
brought Lucy Bertram to live with the Mannerings, thereby
juxtaposing sense and sensibility.

By the time *The Antiquary* was published, the Waverley
novels were familiar to religious families. An advertisement
attached to *The Antiquary,* stating that *Waverley, Guy
Mannering,* and *The Antiquary* were a series, implicitly
invited critics to weigh Scott's achievement in the novel. Put
in the balance, he was not found wanting. Most bona fide
Christians appeared to agree with the *British Critic,* which
said that Scott was "the friend of human kind" and "the
master of every noble, every soft affection of the heart."[19]

19. *British Critic,* 5 (1816), 633.

Chapter 4
The Old Curiosity Shop,
and Legh Richmond's Tracts

By 1850 the novel had become the dominant literary genre. According to Kathleen Tillotson, this had happened because Dickens rushed through "the breach" that Scott made in "the general embargo on novel-reading," becoming the first novelist enjoyed by all classes of British society. That Dickens had done so rested, to a large extent, upon his appeal to readers educated in Sunday Schools and teethed on religious writings. The influence of this moral tradition is elusive, paradoxically because it was so pervasive. But in Dickens' early novels, strict Protestants found a familiar world. Not only were the characters often clearly recognizable moral types, but the form of parts publication itself was almost second nature to "bible Christians" raised on religious narratives.[1]

Although *Pickwick Papers* (1836–38) made Dickens a household name, *The Old Curiosity Shop* (1840–41) cemented the affection between Dickens and his age. Something of an improvisation, the novel grew out of the faltering sales of his weekly miscellany, *Master Humphrey's Clock* (1840–41). *Master Humphrey* initially sold over 70,000 copies;

1. Tillotson, pp. 15–16.

but when the public discovered that it was not going to contain a novel, sales slumped badly. After a hasty conference with his publishers, Dickens began *The Old Curiosity Shop* in the fourth number of the journal. By February 1841 over 100,000 copies of each issue of *Master Humphrey* were being sold. In terms of circulation no novel had ever captured the imagination of the British public as had *The Old Curiosity Shop*.[2]

To some extent the novel's phenomenal sale resulted from its price. An issue of *Master Humphrey* cost only three pence, while a three-volume novel usually cost between a guinea and 31 shillings. In 1821 Scott's *Kenilworth*, for example, cost 31s 6d. However, the low price only partially explained *The Old Curiosity Shop's* amazing popularity. The widespread appeal of the book centered around the heroine, Little Nell. Since Oscar Wilde's quip that one would have to have a heart of stone not to laugh at her death, modernity has treated her scornfully. In contrast she touched the hearts of the early Victorians, causing them to weep when she died. In his biography of Dickens, Edgar Johnson attributed the difference between modern and Victorian reactions to Little Nell to the dissimilar spirits of the ages, writing, "the fact is we live in a different emotional climate from theirs." Perhaps we would come closer to the truth if Mr. Johnson's statement were emended to read "we live in a different religious climate," for Little Nell was the stock heroine of in-

2. For an account of the genesis of *The Old Curiosity Shop*, see Robert Patten's essay "The Story-Weaver at His Loom," in *Dickens The Craftsman*, ed., Robert Partlow, Jr. (Carbondale, 1970).

numerable religious tracts and biographies. Every issue of the *Evangelical Miscellany* contained at least one account of the "Comfortable Experience and Happy Death" of a Little Nell figure. Generations had wept over legions of Wilberforce Smiths who died happily crying "Ah mother, . . . you have been a good mother to me, and I love you with all my heart, and I love God, and I love Jesus Christ, and I love all the good people, and I love angels, and I shall sing hallelujahs."[3]

Dickens' familiarity with religious tracts cannot be proved from his biography. But he did not live in religious isolation; as it would have been difficult for Noah to have ignored the flood, so Dickens would have been hard put not to have been dampened by at least some of the tracts which fell in torrents upon the reading public. Moreover, as a child in Chatham, Dickens attended a Baptist chapel. Recounting the experience in *The Uncommercial Traveller,* he wrote that he was first caught by the crown of his head, then violently scrubbed as a purification for the temple, and finally carried off to be steamed like a potato in the unventilated breath of the powerful Boanerges Boiler and his congregation. Along with memories of "Little Bethel" which served him so well in his writings, Dickens probably took home handfuls of tracts, for

3. The best accounts of contemporary critical and popular reactions to Little Nell are found in George Ford, *Dickens and His Readers* (Princeton, 1955), pp. 55–71; Madeline House and Graham Storey, eds., *The Letters of Charles Dickens 1840–1841* (Oxford, 1969), II, ix–xii; and Edgar Johnson, *Charles Dickens: His Tragedy and Triumph* (New York, 1952), I, 323. *The Youth's Magazine, or Evangelical Miscellany,* 1 (1805), 140.

the Baptists believed in conscientiously sowing "beside all waters the good seed of the kingdom."[4]

But whether or not Dickens had been familiar with religious writings from his childhood or was just susceptible to the literary-theological spirit of his age, the story of Little Nell bore a close resemblance to two of the period's popular tracts: Legh Richmond's *The Dairyman's Daughter* and *The Young Cottager*. Now consigned like Rowland Hill to the outer realms of critical approval, the Reverend Legh Richmond was one of the most popular writers of his day. The circulation of his tracts, William Jones wrote in 1850, "was so general that they found their way to the palace of kings, and entered the hut of the wandering Indian." To Wilberforce's *Practical Christianity*, Richmond owed his evangelicalism, or as he put it "the first sacred impression which I ever received, as to the spiritual nature of the gospel system, the vital character of personal religion, the corruption of the human heart, and the way of salvation by Jesus Christ."[5]

Following Wilberforce's example, Richmond became a worthy laborer in the vineyard and the Religious Tract Society's most popular author. In order to "feed his lambs," Richmond wrote *The Dairyman's Daughter*. By 1828 over four million copies of the tract had been printed, and it had been circulated in nineteen languages and dialects. Richmond himself became a minor celebrity. The Duke of Kent made him his chaplain and Emperor Alexander of Russia

4. Charles Dickens, *The Uncommercial Traveller and Reprinted Pieces* (London, 1958), pp. 83–84. All references to Dickens' works are to the "Oxford Illustrated Dickens." Jones, p. 173.

5. Jones, pp. 73, 77.

presented him with a testimonial ring. Evoking memories of the popularity of Richardson's fictional characters, pilgrims journeyed to the Isle of Wight to visit the graves of Richmond's two famous heroines, the Dairyman's Daughter and the Young Cottager.[6]

To maintain that Dickens used Richmond's tracts as the source of Little Nell's story would be incorrect. Because he stepped in quickly to bolster the faltering sales of *Master Humphrey*, it was, however, initially difficult for Dickens to plan *The Old Curiosity Shop* much in advance of each week's episode. This haste seems to be reflected in the figure of Little Nell. Even when set beside the other "pellucid bodies" in Dickens' gallery of youthful innocents, she is comparatively pale. Because he was under pressure of rapid composition and publication, Dickens did not fashion a strikingly original heroine. Instead, most probably guided by unconscious memories of earlier reading, he plucked a stock character from out of the world of religious tracts and shaped his narrative about her. "The mind of man," Legh Richmond wrote, "is like a moving picture, supplied with objects, not only from contemplation on things present, but from the fruitful sources of recollection and anticipation" (27). Even if Richmond's writings were not the particular fruitful source of Dickens' novel, the parallels between his tracts and *The Old*

6. Rev. Legh Richmond, *Annals of the Poor. A New Edition, Enlarged and Illustrated, with an Introductory Sketch of the Author by the Rev. John Ayre* (London, 1831), pp. xi, xvii–xviii. Published by the Religious Tract Society, this volume contains Richmond's three most popular tracts: "The Dairyman's Daughter," "The African Servant," and "The Young Cottager." By midcentury 1,354,000 copies of the *Annals of the Poor* had been printed.

Curiosity Shop are instructive. Not only do they show us how deep the evangelical tradition ran in the greatest Victorian novelist, but they were also, I think, partly responsible for the phenomenal success of *The Old Curiosity Shop*. Because the novel's heroine was such a readily identifiable type, wary readers knew immediately that Dickens had supplied them with a proper object for contemplation and anticipation, and not "an artful preparation of moral poison."[7]

In describing the slow deaths of young Christians from consumption, both Dickens and Richmond used similar expressions and reached comparable conclusions. At the beginning of *The Young Cottager*, Richmond stressed that God made Little Jane an emblem. "The Lord," Richmond wrote, "once 'called a little child unto him, and set him in the midst of his disciples,' as an emblem of an illustration of his doctrine. But the Lord did more in the case of Little Jane. He not only called *her*, as a child, to show, by a similitude what conversion means; but he also called her by his grace to be a vessel of mercy, and a living witness of that almighty power and love, by which her own heart was turned to God" (188). Likewise, at the beginning of *The Old Curiosity Shop*, Dickens depicted Nell as a partially allegorical figure. After returning from his initial meeting with Nell, the first old gentleman fell asleep and had a dream. On waking, he analyzed it, thinking, "she seemed to exist in a kind of allegory." "It would be a curious speculation to imagine her, in her future life," he thought, "holding her solitary way among a crowd of wild grotesque companions; the only pure, fresh, youthful object in the throng. It would be curious to find—" (13). To

7. *Eclectic Review*, 7 (1817), 309.

build suspense and because he did not know what the ending would be, Dickens left the sentence unfinished. As Nell's story unfolded, however, the novel read a great deal like a tract, and it was soon obvious that Nell herself was a vessel of mercy and a living witness to God's almighty power and love.

Stressing its importance like Mrs. Trimmer, both Dickens and Richmond took Matthew 18:2 as the key to their heroines' emblematic significance: "Verily I say unto you, except ye be converted, and become as little children, ye shall not enter into the kingdom of heaven." According to Dickens' wise old schoolmaster, no good or innocent person—that is, child—was forgotten when he died. Instead he lived on in the better thoughts of those who loved him, and through them played a part in redeeming the world (406). "When Death strikes down the innocent and young," Dickens wrote, "for every fragile form from which he lets the panting spirit free, a hundred virtues rise, in shapes of mercy, charity, and love, to walk the world, and bless it. Of every tear that sorrowing mortals shed on such green graves, some good is born, some gentler nature comes. In the Destroyer's steps there spring up bright creations that defy his power, and his dark path becomes a way of light to Heaven" (544). Little Nell's death, Dickens seemed to hope, would scatter virtues on the desert air; hearts that had aged and hardened would regain their youthful morality, and readers would become like little children and follow the way of light to heaven.

Nell was not alone in her moral significance, for almost all the characters in *The Old Curiosity Shop* were simple generic devices for teaching morality. The physical deformities of

Quilp and Sally Brass jutted out as visible signs of their inward spiritual corruption. Despite his enjoyable *bonhomie*, Dick Swiveller was recognizable as the stock drunkard doomed unless "plucked out of the fire." Paralleling the main plot, Swiveller's reformation provided the novel with a happy subplot. As Little Nell saved her grandfather but died, so the Marchioness, another child, saved Dick and lived to marry him and live happily ever after. As the demonic gambler, Old Trent had appeared in countless moral tales. In Hannah More's *The Gamester*, Tricket stole his wife's last farthing and left his children breadless in order to gamble. Like Nell's grandfather he had once been a good workman. But possessed by gaming, he "spent his hours in greedy wishes, hopes, and fears; in rage, in oaths, and curses over his cards, with the tankard at his side, often drained by the thirsty passion burning in his stomach, and raging in his mind."[8]

In *The Wonderful Advantage of Adventuring in the Lottery!!!* one of Nell's many predecessors, Mary Brown, tried to stop her husband from gambling: "there is indeed, as our Saviour says, but *one thing needful*. What matter whether we be rich or poor in this life, if we get to heaven at last?"[9] For Dickens and Richmond the one thing needful was the spirit of Christianity. Unfortunately, both men thought, too many people "conformed to this world" and were merely "nominal Christians." In accounting for what he believed was a decline in Christianity and concomitantly in morality,

8. *Evangelical Magazine*, 14 (1806), 324. *The Gamester*, Cheap Repository Tracts (London, 1796), pp. 7–8.

9. *The Wonderful Advantage of Adventuring in the Lottery!!!*, Cheap Repository Tracts (London, 1798?), p. 7.

Wilberforce blamed affluence, writing "every where we may actually trace the effects of increasing wealth and luxury." In agreement with this position, Dickens and Richmond romanticized the good qualities of the poor. Like children, the poor were not corrupted by worldly goods and as sentimental primitives were closer to God.[10]

At the beginning of *The Dairyman's Daughter*, Richmond celebrated the virtues of the poor, writing that it was "particularly gratifying to observe how frequently, among the poorer classes of mankind, the sunshine of mercy beams upon the heart, and bears witness to the image of Christ which the spirit of God has impressed thereupon. Among such the sincerity and simplicity of the Christian character appear unencumbered by those obstacles to spirituality of mind and conversation, which too often prove a great hindrance to those who live in the higher ranks." Often, he declared, the "poor man's cottage" was "the palace of God," and he prayed that the poor might become even richer in faith while the rich became poor in spirit (1–2). Implied in this appreciation of the poor and paraphrase of the beatitudes was a criticism of British society. Only when the rich become poor in spirit, or, to continue the Sermon on the Mount, ceased serving God and Mammon, could Christian charity transcend man-made barriers.

Although *The Old Curiosity Shop* was not primarily a critique of British society, the novel, like Richmond's tracts, teemed with examples of the virtuous poor, whose goodness, Dickens wrote, bore the stamp of heaven (281–282). Like-

10. More, *An Estimate of the Religion of the Fashionable World* (Dublin, 1791), p. 230. Wilberforce, *Practical Christianity*, p. 376.

wise looming as man-made spoliation, not only of the natural countryside but also of natural man, the industrial city burned as an inglorious testimony to the evils of serving Mammon instead of God.

In preaching to their readers, both Dickens and Richmond commented on the spiritual condition of Britain, appropriately enough from hilltop pulpits. Urging the blessings of Christianity upon his readers, Richmond juxtaposed what man had made with the Eden-like hills and dales of the Isle of Wight, exclaiming, "How much of the natural beauties of Paradise still remain in the world, although its spiritual character has been so awfully defaced by sin!" (20). In comparison, Little Nell's and Old Trent's rest on a hill outside of London provided Dickens an occasion for a similar sermon. Calling London a Babel, he contrasted it with the paradise of wild flowers, birds, and waving grass which surrounded Nell and Old Trent. To make the contrast clearer, Nell remembered *The Pilgrim's Progress* and told her grandfather that she felt as if they were both Christian and had laid down their troubles (116–117).

Metaphorically the journey of Nell and her grandfather and that of Elizabeth, the Dairyman's Daughter, and her parents were both pilgrims' progresses. As Nell led her grandfather away from sin and to the Celestial City at the cost of her earthly life, so Elizabeth led her parents from sin at the expense of her life. Resembling Nell's grandfather, with white locks, furrowed cheeks, bent shoulders, and a feeble gait, the old dairyman, or "aged pilgrim," as Richmond called him, said that his daughter gave up a good place in order to take care of her parents, with his wife adding that they were ignorant of religion until their daughter brought "Christ Jesus home." Hearing this, Richmond concluded allegorically: "It is a glorious occupation to win souls to Christ, and guide them out of Egyptian bondage through the wilderness into the promised Canaan. Happy are the families who are walking hand in hand together, as pilgrims, towards the heavenly country."[11]

More important than Nell's or Elizabeth's pilgrimage was that experienced by readers as they traveled vicariously with the heroines to the Celestial City. When "a serious Christian" turned his attention "to the barren state of the wilderness" through which he traveled, Richmond wrote, he was forced to "heave a sigh for the sins and sorrows of his fellow-mortals." Sometimes "like a solitary pilgrim," he wept in secret because men did not keep the laws of God. Occasionally, however, he met a fellow traveler whose "spirit" was "congenial" with his own and with whom he could take "sweet counsel." By relating "something of the mercies" of God, they were able to comfort and strengthen each other and thus beguile "the dreariness of the path." As the "happy experiences of divine consolations" cheered their souls, their sympathies enlarged and the desert appeared to blossom "as the rose" (175–176). The books of both Dickens and Richmond focused each reader's attention on the barren wilderness through which he was traveling and on the plight of his fellow mortals. Each introduced a fictional traveling companion, whose spirit, if not immediately congenial with the reader's, was at least morally elevated and inspirational. From Little Nell and Elizabeth, the reader could learn some-

11. Richmond, pp. 10, 21, 78.

thing of God's mercy and kindness. Not only would the stories beguile the dreariness of his path, but hopefully they would comfort and strengthen him and expand his sympathies, so that when he approached the gate of the Celestial City with the young pilgrims, happy experiences of consolation would fill his mind and the desert would appear to blossom as the rose.

Before they entered the Celestial City, Elizabeth and Nell became similarly angelic. Over Elizabeth's face, Richmond wrote, "the peace of God, which passeth all understanding, had cast a triumphant calm" (87). Of Little Nell, Dickens wrote, "a change had been gradually stealing over her, in the time of her loneliness and sorrow. With failing strength and heightening resolution, there had sprung up a purified and altered mind; there had grown in her bosom blessed thoughts and hopes, which are the portion of few but the weak and drooping " (388). For the "serious Christian" Death had no sting; and as Elizabeth lay dying, Richmond turned to her mother and said ecstatically, "what mercy to have a child so near heaven as yours is!" (88). Although perhaps less subtle, Richmond's sentiment did not differ much from that of Dickens' pious schoolmaster who asked Nell's mourners: "Think what earth is, compared with the World to which her young spirit has winged its early flight; and say, if one deliberate wish expressed in solemn terms above this bed could call her back to life, which of us would utter it?" (539). After death even the bodies of Little Nell and Elizabeth were similarly adorned. Nell's couch was dressed with "winter berries and green leaves"(539), while Elizabeth was covered with fading flowers that reminded Richmond "of that Paradise whose flowers are immortal, and where her never-dying soul is at rest" (101).

Equally inspirational was Richmond's story of Little Jane, a twelve-year-old cottager. Cut from the same moral and narrative cloth as that of Nell, Little Jane's life was "short but not useless," for it similarly effected "a work of mercy" in readers' hearts (220). Richmond first met Little Jane at his Saturday afternoon Bible class. Then, he related, since the churchyard bordered his garden, he did not have far to look "for subjects of warning and exhortation" suitable to his "little flock." The churchyard became a "book of instruction, and every gravestone a leaf of edification," as he sent the children to memorize the epitaphs on tombstones (181–182). Grim as Richmond's visual aids may seem to modern sensibilities, they were orthodox and respectable devices for teaching children about "the resurrection and the life."

"The language of the silent tombs" had long played an important part in religious writings. In *No Fiction*, for example, when Lefevre visited his mother in the country for the first time in seven years, he learned that his childhood sweetheart had died recently. When he visited her grave, both he and the readers who expected Reed's book to be just another comfortable "moral tale" were momentarily jarred out of their complacent faiths by the epitaph I FOUND REDEMPTION THROUGH THE BLOOD OF THE LAMB: READER, HAST THOU?[12]

12. Reed, *No Fiction* (London, 1819), I, 75. *Methodist Magazine*, 21 (1798), 140. See the Graveyard School of poetry, including Thomas Parnell's "A Night-Piece on Death," Edward Young's "Night Thoughts," Robert Blair's "The Grave," and Thomas Gray's "Elegy Written in a Country Churchyard."

Chapter 4

For Dickens the graveyard also served as an appropriate book of instruction. Soon after reaching the haven of the schoolmaster's restful village, Nell began to clear the ground around the graves of children. Here Nell, and Dickens' readers as they turned among the tombs with her, learned to put death into a Christian perspective. On first seeing the village, Nell called it "a quiet, happy place—a place to live and learn to die in" (386). Carefully detailing her conversations with the sexton, the schoolmaster, and the little boy, Dickens showed Nell learning how to die happily. At the beginning of *The Young Cottager*, Jane memorized a consoling epitaph she found on Mr. B——'s headstone." Teaching her how to live for a happy death, it read: "Hail glorious Gospel! heavenly light, whereby / we live with comfort, and with comfort die; / and view beyond this gloomy scene, the tomb, / A life of endless happiness to come" (187, 200).

While she tended the ground about the children's graves, Little Nell had the leisure to grow wise and learn the meaning of Mr. B's epitaph. At her death the schoolmaster said that justice did not end on earth, implying that after a life of hardships Nell would enjoy endless happiness (539). As Nell's grandfather had been the immediate cause of her sufferings, so the parents and friends of "poor Jenny" had caused her mortal anxieties by making game of her reading "the Bible so much" (191). At the "affecting moment" of her death, however, she received immortal restitution when "the rays of the morning sun darted into the room," filling Richmond's imagination with "the significant emblem of 'the tender mercy of God' " and implying that her soul had risen to heaven (252). Similarly, the last illustration in *The Old Curiosity Shop* showed Little Nell wrapped safely in the arms of angels and ascending to heaven in a beam of light.

After outlining his characters' future lives, Dickens echoed the ninth verse of Psalm 90: "Such are the changes which in a few years bring about, and so do things pass away, like a tale that is told" (555). Emphasizing that man's life span was limited, Psalm 90 begs God to "teach *us* to number our days, that we may apply *our* hearts unto wisdom." Like Richmond's tracts, *The Old Curiosity Shop* was meant to be a book of wisdom, touching its readers' hearts and teaching them how to live. Richmond, as Dickens' spirited kinsman, also admonished his readers, to ensure that they would not miss his wisdom and would learn to number their days. Less artistically but with Dickens' sense of urgency, Richmond asked: "My *poor* reader, the Dairyman's daughter was a *poor* girl, and the child of a *poor* man. Herein thou resemblest her: But dost thou resemble *her*, as she resembled Christ? Art thou made *rich* by faith? Hast thou a crown laid up for thee? Is thine heart set upon heavenly riches? If not, read this story once more, and then pray earnestly for like precious faith" (104–105).

To argue that Dickens was at one with the world of evangelical tracts in a novel in which Little Bethel squats as a visible criticism of evangelicalism may seem as crooked a bit of reasoning as the very streets by which that "obnoxious conventicle" was approached (305). But the predominant quality of Dickens' imagination was that his heart and mind were often at odds. Where his mind went, his heart was not sure to follow. And in *The Old Curiosity Shop*, while his mind criticized the evangelicalism of Little Bethel's consecrated cobbler, his heart was far away with Little Nell, treading in Legh Richmond's footsteps through "the barren state of the wilderness."

Chapter 5
Protestantism in
Barnaby Rudge

Barnaby Rudge followed
The Old Curiosity Shop in the pages of *Master Humphrey*.
Lacking a "Nelliad," a pilgrimage-like unity, the novel has
never been popular, and most students of Dickens have
agreed with Edgar Johnson's statement that *Barnaby Rudge*
with its "clumsy and broken-backed plot" was "the least
satisfactory of all Dickens's full length books." After granting *Barnaby's* low standing in the Dickens canon, Kathleen
Tillotson perceptively observed, however, that the novel had
"a remarkable unity of feeling." Based not upon a narrative
device, such as the dust in *Our Mutual Friend* or the prisons
in *Little Dorrit,* this unity rests solidly on the moral tradition. Permeated by the morality taught in Sunday Schools
and by the message of religious tracts and periodicals, *Barnaby Rudge* is the most theologically revealing of Dickens'
early novels. In its pages evangelical Protestantism received
the fullest and most sympathetic treatment that Dickens
ever gave it. As a result the novel provides valuable insights
into not only Dickens' religious beliefs but also the literary
history of the moral tradition.[1]

1. Johnson, I, 330. Kathleen Tillotson, *Barnaby Rudge* (London,
1954), xii.

If the *Pickwick Papers* had not been so successful, *Barnaby Rudge*, then projected as *Gabriel Vardon, the Locksmith of London*, would have been Dickens' first novel. After *Pickwick*, however, a complicated series of events prevented Dickens from writing the book until 1841. When it finally appeared, *Barnaby* had fermented in Dickens' imagination for five years. After such a long delay, the novel's publication testified to the strong hold the story had on Dickens. Not surprisingly, midway through the book Dickens wrote Forster that he was "in great heart and spirits with the story."[2] This simple statement is important to our understanding of the novel. Since the book revealed his religious attitudes, *Barnaby Rudge* touched Dickens in a way that his earlier novels had not, with the possible exception of *The Old Curiosity Shop*.

Ostensibly *Barnaby Rudge* appears to be an attack on evangelical Protestantism. As parish clerk, Solomon Daisy was the Maypole's ludicrous "representative of church and state" (10). Echoing the fervor of itinerant preachers, the wind howled like a Christian (250). Immersed in the Protestant Manual, Mrs. Varden mouthed evangelical cant, while hypocritical self-seekers such as Miggs and Gashford hid their worldly aims under the cloak of Protestant nonconformity. Sheltered by the "moral" cry of "No Popery," the London mob satanically created an earthly hell. All this, however, was a critique of the abuses of Protestantism, epitomized by the followers of Lord George Gordon. The turmoil brought about by Gordon's adherents did not discredit right Protestant practice. Instead the riots illustrated the

2. Tillotson, p. vi.

dangers of neglecting Christian benevolence and indirectly urged readers to examine the Christian basis of their own faiths.

The primary biblical text behind the novel was 2 Corinthians 3:6: "The letter killeth, but the spirit giveth life," a text Dickens would return to in all his novels. Standing on the letter of religion, Mrs. Varden distorted the charitable basis of Protestantism. Under the influence of Miggs, who said she despised her fellow creatures "as every practicable Christian should" (105), Mrs. Varden misunderstood the doctrine of original sin. Instead of fragmenting the Christian community and impeding good works, original sin supported the brotherhood of man and furnished the Christian with a rationale for good deeds.

In 1794 the *Evangelical Magazine* wrote that "private self-love" denied original sin and was "the grand succedaneum in human affections to the love of God and man." While this prevailed, the journal said, "the creature assumes the place of the Creator, and seeks his own gratification, honour, and interest, as the ultimate end of all his actions." In contrast the doctrine of original sin led to "the truest benevolence," because it convinced men of their brotherhood and responsibility for one another.[3]

It is doubtful, however, that Dickens accepted this view of original sin as the basis of man's humanity to man. Even in the 1790's the *Evangelical Magazine* thought it necessary to explain repeatedly the interdependence of benevolence and original sin. "It has sometimes been objected to this doctrine," the journal wrote in 1793, "that it tends to en-

3. *Evangelical Magazine*, 1 (1793), 73; 2 (1794), 96.

courage an ill opinion of our fellow-creatures; and that the very admission of such a sentiment seems to indicate a malignant and censorious disposition. But when we consider ourselves as involved in the same charge with other men, the humbling sense of our own depravity must prove an antidote to all improper harshness and severity towards our fellow-sinners: And if we are fully satisfied of the fact, it must be an evidence of the truest benevolence, to labour to convince mankind of their criminality." But 1841 was not 1793. Despite the fact that there were more tracts than ever and Sunday Schools taught more students, polemical evangelicalism was not in its prime. In particular the Church of England was shifting back toward latitudinarianism. Sydney Smith, in the preface to his works in 1839, wrote that the changes in human affairs were strange and ludicrous. Liberality, he observed, was now a lucrative business, and whoever had an institution to destroy had his fortune made.[4]

Acutely aware of the danger of Miggs-like interpretations of the letter for the spirit of Christianity, Dickens rejected original sin as the basis of good deeds. Paradoxically, though, the doctrine seemed to lie behind his authoritarianism and admiration for the police and mysterious men of action like Bucket and Nadgett. In *Practical Christianity*, Wilberforce argued that man was "tainted with sin, not slightly and superficially, but radically and to the very core." Believing that "depravity" was always present even in the best of men, Wilberforce held that strict laws were necessary to the survival of the state. Both religiously and socially, man had to be kept on "the path of righteousness." If he were not, Wil-

4. Ibid., 1 (1793), 72. Sydney Smith, *Works* (London, 1839), I, ix.

berforce declared, men would become animals, and revolution would break out in Britain.[5]

In *Barnaby Rudge* Gordon's abuse and concomitant undermining of orthodox Protestantism led to chaos. Like Old Testament prophecies, Dickens' descriptions of the mob stemmed from the same source as Wilberforce's conservatism: the belief that an Hebraic authoritarianism was necessary to preserve civilization. Without discipline, men became beasts; and emblematically, lurid flames, dust, and smoke billowed through *Barnaby* as the rabble vented its "maniac rage" (525). Once the army, almost an embodiment of Hebraic law, asserted itself, order was restored; and men became human again.

Dickens' interesting and significant stance on original sin was but the tip of the religious iceberg under *Barnaby Rudge*. Protestantism was also the source of Dickens' radicalism, illustrated by his celebration of sturdy yeomen like John Grueby and his scorn for hierarchies represented by the Lord Mayor, Sir John Chester, and "a country gentleman of the true school" (357). Holding that every man could speak directly to God and wrestle for his salvation like Jacob in the desert with the angel, evangelical Protestantism was revolutionary by implication. During the Napoleonic Wars, this had been recognized, and a great cry had been raised against nonconformists who promoted the "levelling system of equality."[6] But by 1841 successive waves of Cumberland Beggars, *Village Dialogues*, and *Methodist Magazines* had greatly

5. Wilberforce, pp. 26–27, 32.
6. T. E. Owen, *Methodism Unmasked, or the Progress of Puritanism from the Sixteenth to the Nineteenth Century* (London, 1802), p. 75.

eroded the remnants of such feudal trappings as social degree and ecclesiastical hierarchy.

Despite his frequent attacks on religious cant, many of Dickens' stands in *Barnaby Rudge* parroted evangelical positions. In the novel he directly or indirectly attacked drunkenness, masquerades, fashionable education, and undisciplined reading—all anathemas to strict Protestants. On the *Evangelical Magazine*'s Spiritual Barometer, marking "the progress of SIN and GRACE," at — 30 was the theater, Vauxhall, and "much wine and spirits." At — 50 in the heady company of profaneness and adultery were masquerades. Like the Barometer, Dickens thought masquerades corrupted youth. In *Barnaby Rudge* he obliquely criticized them by having innocent Emma Haredale attend one against her will. Moreover, in order to inform her of Edward Chester's wound, Gabriel Varden, Dickens' ideal Christian, disapprovingly searched the masquerade for her (36). While there, he felt ill at ease; indirectly, Dickens seemed to say, a masquerade was no place for a Christian.[7]

Dickens' attitude toward drink also resembled that implied by the Barometer. Neither Dickens nor rigorous Protestants disapproved of spirits. In raising his brown Toby jug, Gabriel Varden used rather than abused the fruits of the earth. In terms of the Barometer, his drinking was never "much" and did not lead to drunkenness. Likewise the comfortable Maypole, with young Joe Willet as owner, resembled the *Cheap Repository's* ideal inn, run by an "honest publican." Spreading responsibility along with good cheer, like Joe, the

7. *Evangelical Magazine*, 8 (1800), 526.

honest publican was soon "in a fair way of becoming one of the most opulent inn-keepers in that part of the country."[8] In contrast to moderate drinking, drunkenness turned Hugh and the London mob into animals. Furthermore, by encouraging Hugh to drink excessively, Sir John Chester was a demonic publican, neglecting his moral responsibility for his fellows in order to get them in his power by playing upon their weaknesses.

Believing that the "unprincipled and ignorant" human mind was "exposed to every vicious and injurious sentiment, like an uncultivated field without a fence," Sunday School theorists emphasized the importance of a structured religious education. Particularly galling, not only because of its supposed lack of religious instruction but also because of implied social discrimination, was what evangelicals labeled "fashionable education." Typifying criticism of fashionable education was Mr. Worthy's lecture to Mr. Lovely in the *Village Dialogues*. "You cannot be ignorant of the style of education among young persons of rank," Mr. Worthy expostulated, "Look at the plain, honest, country milk-maid; next contrast her with the vain baubles turned out, not only from the families of too many of the Right Honourables of the day, but from most of our modern boarding schools: these from being first mere babies, afterwards got something above it as they grew up towards child-hood; then they are sent to these destructive places of female education, where they are a second time reduced almost, to a state of baby-

8. *The Honest Publican,* Cheap Repository Tracts (London, 1797), p. 15.

hood; and in this fools paradise, they seem happy to live through all their lives, fifty times more offensive babies, than if they had never left their cradles."[9]

In 1805 the *Christian Observer* asked typically if the end of fashionable education was to make young people "followers of the meek and lowly Jesus." Was it, the *Observer* questioned, "to prepare them for the society of saints and angels, by bringing them up in the nurture and admonition of the Lord, teaching them to remember and to fear their Creator in the days of their youth, and thus forming and training them to such rules of judgement, and such a course of life, as the laws and precepts of the Bible require?" To answer the question "affirmatively would," the *Observer* concluded, "be mere mockery."[10]

In full agreement with this position, Dickens preached the dangers of fashionable education. Having received such an education, Edward Chester was "fit for nothing" (116). Only his good angel, in the person of Emma Haredale, and his childlike innocence (120) prevented his becoming an amoral fortune hunter. Edward's resemblance to a child was, of course, extremely important. Again Dickens stressed that one had to resemble a child in order to gain the kingdom of heaven. Young Chester, true to his own feelings, was cut from the same moral cloth as Dickens' naturals—Kit Nubbles and Mr. Toots, for example. Kit was unable to write, and in Mr. Toots's case the thematic parallel was striking. "Blowing" (becoming a simpleton) before his time, Mr. Toots did not

9. *Evangelical Magazine*, 1 (1793), 283. Rowland Hill, *Village Dialogues* (London, 1803), III, 67.

10. *Christian Observer*, 4 (1805), 43.

become one of Blimber's "young Chesterfields."[11] Correspondingly fashionable education failed to make Edward a caricature of Lord Chesterfield like his father.

Even more conventional than the attack on fashionable education was Dickens' "Andrew Reedish" criticism of undisciplined reading. Like that of Waverley, Sim Tapperwit's disasterously absurd behavior resulted from an unhealthy regimen of books which gave him "false views of human life" and taught "contempt for humble and domestic duties; for industry, frugality, and retirement." The ritual of the Prentice Knights was not so much a parody of masonic hocuspocus as it was an amalgam taken from gothic novels and swashbuckling romances—in short, novels of sensibility.[12]

Like Hannah More, Dickens used the characters of *Barnaby Rudge* as pawns in theological discussions. Almost equivalent to degree marks on the Spiritual Barometer, each main character represented a step on the road from Perdition to Glory. At opposite ends of the barometer were Gabriel Varden and Sir John Chester. In between were, most importantly, Mrs. Varden, Barnaby, Mary Rudge, Old Rudge, Hugh, and Geoffrey Haredale. Dickens' ideal Christian was Gabriel Varden, whose unobtrusive moral character could be equally well described by Samuel Clarke or the *Methodist Magazine*. "The Great and Principal Design of every man's life," Clarke wrote, "ought to be promoting the Glory of God, the encouraging of Virtue, and discouraging every kind of Vice. Not that any man is obliged to be perpetually employed in actions

11. *Dombey and Son* (London, 1950), p. 203.
12. More, *The Two Wealthy Farmers*, Cheap Repository Tracts (London, 1795), Pt. I, 20.

Chapter 5

that are *immediately* of a religious nature; or that all his
Thoughts and Discourses are to be wholly confined to things
Sacred: But that his Principal and Final Aim, his General
and Constant View, the settled Temper and Disposition of
his mind, and the Habitual Tendency of all his Actions, be
the establishing of Truth and Right in the World." In 1798
the *Methodist Magazine* said that Christian law was summed
up under two heads: "the Love of God, and the Love of our
Neighbour." For Andrew Reed the divine principle consisted
of *"love towards God"* and *"benevolence towards men"* and
was directly opposed to "vanity, pride, enmity, and selfishness."[13] Thus, for example, Varden pressed Sir John to help
Hugh in prison. Similarly when Joe told him that he was
considering leaving the Maypole and trusting to chance, the
locksmith quietly replied that chance was a bad thing to
trust, implying that Joe should put his trust in the Lord (25).

Encouraging readers to note the discrepancy between appearance and reality or the difference between the letter and
the spirit of Christianity, Dickens made Varden appear weak.
This was however, deceptive, as readers soon learned, for
Varden's domestic patience resulted not from impotence
but from traditional Christian virtue. Preaching brotherhood, the *Methodist Magazine*, quoting from I Peter, 3: 8–9,
which urged readers to have "compassion one of another;
love as brethren, be pitiful, be courteous: Not rendering evil
for evil, or railing for railing; but contrariwise, blessing."[14]
Showing that Varden's patience stemmed from strength

13. Clarke, I, 238. *Methodist Magazine*, 21 (1798), 149; 23 (1800), 374.
Reed, II, 216.
14. *Methodist Magazine*, 21 (1798), 149.

rather than weakness, Dickens made him a latter-day Abdiel, having him dare the wrath of the mob by refusing to open Newgate.

Varden's right religion strengthened him during the riots, whereas his wife's imperfect faith offered her no support. Mrs. Varden, not understanding Christian charity, actually and metaphorically gave alms to a bad cause. In the *Cheap Repository Tracts*, the evangelical view of charity was summed up simply: "Charity . . . may very well exist without alms-giving. It consists in *benevolence of heart*, in the endeavour to assist one's fellow creatures, and to make all happy around one."[15] Systematizing the spirit out of Christianity and thereby fragmenting the community, the Protestant Manual was the source of Mrs. Varden's errors. Study of the Manual made one a Miggs, whose angular body and sharp face were outward and visible signs of her constricted spiritual nature.

In criticizing religious self-help manuals, Dickens implicitly urged his readers to return to Christian fundamentals, traditionally found in the Bible. More explicit than *Barnaby Rudge* but similar in spirit, a writer in the *Evangelical Magazine* in 1796 told subscribers to read the Bible instead of popular studies of religion. "Here let us drink of the celestial fountain," he wrote, "until our hearts be replenished, our minds animated, and our souls really benefited." Likewise in a popular novel, *Sancho, or the Proverbialist* (1816), John Cunningham illustrated the dangers of living by the letter rather than the spirit of Christianity. Cunningham's

15. *Sweep, Soot O!! Some Account of Little Jem, the Chimney Sweeper and His Benefactress*, Cheap Repository Tracts (London, 1797?), p. 5.

criticism of his hero's faith was motivated by a moral imperative similar to the one that created Mrs. Varden. Built on
maxims, the religion of Sancho and Mrs. Varden, and by
implication that of many nineteenth-century Christians, was
imperfect. The "humble design," of *Sancho*, Cunningham
wrote, was to show "that a large portion of the most popular
maxims are exceedingly unsafe—that many of them have a
strong tendency to create a sordid and selfish character—that
our principles of action are to be sought in the Bible—and,
finally, that if any person desires to be singularly happy, he
has only to pray and to labour to become eminently good."[16]
If we broaden Cunningham's maxims to include institutions
that had lost their moral spirit (*Dombey and Son*'s dust-
filled churches and *Little Dorrit*'s Circumlocution Office),
then we have much of the "humble design" of Dickens' later
novels.

Dickens often described man's struggle to be good in meta-
phoric terms. Thus Dick Swiveller and Eugene Wrayburn became ill. Emblematically, good and evil struggled for mastery
in their breasts, with the result that through suffering both
men atoned for their sins and were spiritually reborn. Although Mrs. Varden did not become ill, her reformation was
brought about through suffering. To paraphrase Wordsworth, a deep distress christianized her soul. Early in the
novel Dickens prepared readers for her change, writing that
her neighbors thought "a tumble down some half-dozen
rounds in the world's ladder . . . would be the making of her"

16. *Evangelical Magazine*, 4 (1796), 24. Cunningham, *Sancho, or the
Proverbialist* (London, 1816), pp. 180–181.

(54). Tumbling her down, the riots shattered Mrs. Varden's selfishness. Rejecting the narrow maxim-filled Protestant Manual, she embraced the broader spirit of Christianity and, divesting herself "of every degree of bitterness, unkindness, enmity," was restored "to that rectitude of mind in which we were created." In Mrs. Varden's restoration, religious readers recognized the didactic stuff out of which religious magazines were made. With a fervent ingredient of purple prose, A.B. described his change of heart in the *Christian Mirror*, writing "in every worldly path my feet were pierced with thorns, clouds of darkness were before my eyes wherever I turned them, whatever I grasped it broke like a bubble in my hand. God, dwelling in Christ, appeared to be the only ark where my feet could rest—the only sun that could enlighten my darkness."[17]

As Gabriel Varden was the ideal Christian, so Sir John Chester was the novel's fallen man of the world. In caricaturing Lord Chesterfield, Dickens evoked an automatic response from evangelical readers. For such readers, Chesterfield was the archetypical Belial who could make the worse appear the better cause. Denying the love of God which led to love of man, Chester loved the world. "It is the *undue* and *inordinate* affection to the things of this life," the *Evangelical Magazine* wrote in 1793, "which the divine word forbids."[18] For Dickens an inordinate love for things led a man to lose his soul and thereby himself become a dead thing. Thus Sarah

17. *Methodist Magazine*, 21 (1798), 151–152, 201. *Christian Mirror*, 1 (1805), 6.
18. *Evangelical Magazine*, 1 (1793), 105.

Gamp became her old clothes, and Silas Wegg, his amputated leg.

In quarrelling with Sir John, Edward said he knew his father's creed (243). Edward was not alone in his knowledge. For over fifty years evangelicals had attacked Lord Chesterfield's creed, as the epitome of a worldly code of conduct. In 1776 the *Gospel Magazine* printed "Christianity Reversed: or, A New Office of Initiation, for all Youths of the Superior Class. Being a Summary of Lord Chesterfield's Creed." Pinpointing evangelical objections to worldly conduct, "Christianity Reversed" not only tells us a great deal about evangelical views of the fashionable world but also sheds light on Dickens' Protestantism. The ethical criticism behind the irony of the *Gospel Magazine* lay behind Dickens' picture of Sir John. "I believe," the writer for the journal wrote, "that this world is the object of my hopes and morals; and that the little prettinesses of life will answer all the ends of human existence. I believe that we are to succede in all things, by the *graces* of civility and attention; that there is no sin, but against good manners; and that all religion and virtue consist in outward appearance. I believe, that all women are children, and all men fools; except a few cunning people, who see through the rest, and make their use of them. I believe, that hypocrisy, fornication, and adultery, are within the lines of morality: that a woman may be honourable when she has lost her honour, and virtuous when she has lost her virtue. This, and whatever else is necessary to obtain my own ends, and bring me into repute, I resolve to follow; and to avoid all moral offences: such as scratching my head before company, spitting upon the floor, and omitting to pick up a Lady's fan. And in this persuasion I will persevere, without any regard to the resurrection of the body or the life everlasting. *Amen.*"[19]

The creed was followed by a short catechism in which the child was named "A Fine Gentleman." Then the catechist said "I introduce thee to the world, the flesh, and the devil, that thou mayest triumph over all awkwardness, and grow up in all politeness; that thou mayest be acceptable to the Lady's, celebrated for refined breeding, able to speak French and read Italian . . . get into Parliament." Finally the catechist addressed the youth's sponsor: "Ye are to take care that this child, when he is of a proper age, be brought to the C——t, to be *confirmed.*"

The *Gospel Magazine's* heavy-handed didacticism ought not to divert us from the significance of "Christianity Reversed." The creed contained the seeds of Sir John Chester. Like "A Fine Gentleman" Sir John intimately knew the world, the flesh, and the devil. Furthermore he triumphed over awkwardness, grew up in politeness, was acceptable to "Lady's," and obtained a seat in Parliament. Denying the value of religion except as a device to be used with advantage by cunning men, he believed success depended entirely upon the graces. He said that although a mere king or queen could make a Lord, "only the Devil himself—and the Graces" could "make a Chesterfield" (174).

To ensure that readers would not overlook the errors of

19. *Gospel Magazine,* 3 (1776), 487–489.

Sir John's ways, Dickens intruded into the narrative to preach short sermons on several occasions. One of these stressed God's presence in the natural world. Brought up on Anna Barbauld's *Hymns*, generations of Protestants had been taught "every field" was "like an open book," "every painted flower" had "a lesson written on its leaves," and "every murmuring brook" had "a tongue." Only the "child of reason" could not sense God's presence in the world about him.[20] Riding to the Maypole on a day when "the trees were budding into leaf, the hedges and grass were green, the air was musical with songs of birds," Sir John was just such a child of reason, oblivious to the God about him. For Dickens he was a worldly man, held to the earth "by a moral law of gravitation." Looking at the spangled sky, he did not see such "heavenly constellations as Charity, Forbearance, Universal Love, and Mercy" (217).

After admitting that "Shakespeare was undoubtedly very fine in his way" and Milton "good, though prosy," Sir John said that the "writer who should be his country's pride" was Lord Chesterfield (173). For Dickens, it was not a matter of *should;* within the world of *Barnaby Rudge* and, by extension nineteenth-century Britain, Chesterfield was his country's pride. Society wrongly admired their Sir Johns and made them members of Parliament while neglecting the quietly virtuous Gabriel Vardens.

In *The Infidel Father* (1802), Mrs. West warned her readers against the seductive appearance of "false principles." The manners of the villain, Lord Glanville, she wrote, "were formed in the school of Chesterfield." "Corrected by the

20. Barbauld, pp. 39, 75.

opinions of the world, and restrained by prudential and interested motives," Glanville so disguised his "poison" that it
was easy for him to pour it into "unwary ears."[21] In *Barnaby
Rudge* the infidel father—mild, cherubic Chester—poured
poison into the ears of Mrs. Varden and John Willet, who
because of their flawed faiths were unable to understand the
difference between good and evil. By undermining love and
the family, Chester struck not only at the basis of Christianity but also at the political stability of Great Britain.

Pressing upon his countrymen the necessity of distinguish-
ing appearance from reality, Dickens depicted Sir John as a
malignant source of evil. Like Milton in *Paradise Lost*, he
stressed the discrepancy between his Satan's deeds and his
appearance. For Dickens and the *Gospel Magazine* honor
and virtue were only possible if Christianity formed the cor-
nerstone of society. In his *Practical Christianity*, Wilberforce
argued that religion promoted "the temporal well-being of
political communities."[22] Agreeing, Dickens used Hugh's biography as a parable, showing how Chesterfield's creed was
responsible for chaos. Through the institution of holy matri-
mony, Christianity attempted to discipline the destructive
tendencies of man's animal energies and to transform them
into creative energies. Within the moral order provided by
the structure of a Christian family, selfishness ideally became
selflessness as individuals assumed responsibility for and
cared for the needs of others. In *Barnaby Rudge* the family
was a microcosm of British society. When harmony prevailed
within families, as it did at the end of the novel, the nation

21. West, *The Infidel Father* (London, 1802), I, ii, 144–145.
22. Wilberforce, p. 364.

was calm. Likewise disorder within families was paralleled by national disturbances. And when the acts of an individual threatened the institution of marriage, and thereby the family, the nation itself was threatened. Thus Sir John's begetting Hugh outside marriage was fraught with macrocosmic implications. As Sir John had thrown off the restraints of Christianity, given free rein to his animal energies, and sired a bestial son who spread destruction wherever he went, so the London mob had similarly thrown off Christianity, and loosing their animal energies during the Gordon riots had created a city of fiery and dreadful night. When Hugh appeared at the center of the riots, it was metaphorically fitting, for Hugh, like the mob, could exist only after Christian standards of right behavior had been undermined.

Dickens believed that a truly Christian community based on the brotherhood of man would have prevented Hugh from becoming an animal. For Dickens the society that refused to recognize the brotherhood of all men and assume responsibility for others sowed the seeds of its own dissolution. In *Barnaby Rudge* John Willet was the voice of the irresponsible community. On first meeting Hugh in the novel, the reader immediately notices the disparity between Hugh's handsome, athletic figure and "the disorder of the whole man" (86). Thinking Hugh more animal than man, Willet said that if Hugh had a soul, it was "such a very small one" that it did not influence his actions (97). Not able to read or write, Hugh was an animal, Willet stated, because his father had not drawn out his "faculties." Now, Willet said, it was too late, and one could do nothing except treat Hugh as an animal (86–87). Ironically, of course, Sir John did draw

out Hugh's lower faculties by encouraging his riotous ac-
tivities; more important, however, was Willet's implicit denial of man's Christian responsibility for men, a denial that
eventually led to the sacking of the Maypole. For Dickens,
Hugh represented the inarticulate and areligious English
masses. His handsome face and powerful physique were signs
of his potential for good. But under the tutelage of a corrupt
"fine gentleman," represented by Sir John, and suffering from
the unchristian neglect of the middle classes, Hugh was often
a source of destruction. If something were not done for the
Hughs of England by the smug John Willets, then, Dickens
implied, disorder and revolution were inevitable.

For Dickens and religious people, the "one thing needful"
was Christianity. It would care for, then tame, the beast in
Hugh, and by developing his better nature would enlarge
his soul and order "the disorder of the whole man." The poor
law riots, the Chartist Movement, the mass meetings on Ker-
sal Moor and Kennington Common, all lay, as Mrs. Tillotson tells us, behind *Barnaby Rudge*. With these events in
mind Dickens meant Hugh's story to illustrate the dangers
of neglecting the spirit of Christianity. In the same evangelical vein, the Reverend William Turner recommended Sunday Schools in 1786 as the best means of spreading religion
and putting out the flames of disorder which he thought
threatened to engulf the nation. Concerns similar to those
which led to Hugh's creation charged Turner's peroration.
"Can we wonder," Turner asked, "that our persons and
properties are growing daily less secure from the violent attacks of the idle and debauched? And while we shudder at
the horrid scenes which are acting perpetually in the neigh-

bourhood of the metropolis, and at the monthly sacrifice of multitudes to the ineffectual cruelty of sanguinary laws, can we forbear to form the most alarming apprehensions, lest the evil should spread in its full extent into the most distant provinces, till, the measure of our iniquities being filled up, the avenging justice of the Almighty shall strike the name of Britain out of the catalogue of nations!"[23] To many people's minds, the religious enthusiasm that was responsible for the Sunday Schools had prevented violent upheavals from occurring in Britain in the latter part of the eighteenth century. Now through the medium of *Barnaby Rudge*, Dickens called for a similar rebirth of Christian activism.

By being easily recognizable as either good or evil, the flat characters of *Barnaby Rudge* contributed to the book's "remarkable unity of feeling." Unfortunately, Barnaby's character was inconsistent, with the result that he often seemed out of place in the novel and impeded the story's didacticism. Sometimes Dickens described Barnaby as a type of "nature's simple child." Not strapped into an identity by the letter of the Protestant Manual or a worldly code of manners, Barnaby was free to travel throughout London and the surrounding countryside and serve as a link between diverse elements of English society. Moreover with a "complete and lasting" childhood (190), Barnaby, the friend of animals and beggars alike, had a spontaneity of consciousness which Dickens implied was necessary if one were to inherit the kingdom of heaven. Singing his prayers in the straw, Barnaby often seemed the prelapsarian holy innocent, living in the manger, true to the spirit rather than the law of Christianity.

23. Tillotson, *Barnaby*, p. vii. Turner, p. 15.

The picture of a Christian innocent happily trailing clouds of glory clashed with the old Testament description of an unfortunate youth suffering because of the sins of his father. Behind the inconsistency lay an ambivalent attitude toward original sin and the concept of the soul. At the beginning of the novel the red birthmark on Barnaby's wrist was seemingly an outward sign of original sin (41). However, Dickens also emphasized at the first of the book that Barnaby did not have a soul. According to orthodox Protestant theology, the soul alone distinguished man from the brutes and enabled him to resemble God. Without a soul it was impossible for a creature to be human and, consequently, impossible to suffer from original sin. Clearly, Barnaby was not simply an animal, but then neither was he entirely human. After carefully stressing the importance of the fact that Barnaby lacked a soul, however, Dickens abruptly dropped the matter. And subsequently Barnaby wandered through the book in a variety of roles. Sometimes he resembled a holy child; other times he seemed like a wild animal, or, on occasions, a man broken down by the burden of sin. At the conclusion of the novel, when he was hurriedly tying together the loose ends of the narrative, Dickens inexplicably reintroduced the subject and implied that the elder Rudge's death had enabled Barnaby to grow beyond his earlier mental and spiritual limitations. Barnaby, he said, grew "more rational" and "had a better memory and greater steadiness of purpose." Unfortunately "a dark cloud," Dickens wrote, "overhung his whole previous existence, and never cleared away" (633–634). When viewed in theological context, the dark cloud is comparable to original sin. "Soon as reason dawns," the *Evangel-*

ical Magazine wrote, "the seeds of corruption appear."[24] If the dark cloud was original sin, the corruption that appeared simultaneously with reason, then what was the red birthmark? Or why did the death of his father contribute to the improvement of Barnaby's reason and memory? Did Barnaby somehow gain a soul after his father's death? And if he did, why did the being without a soul seemingly suffer periodically throughout the novel from something resembling original sin? When taken as a whole, the world of Dickens' novels is wonderfully inconsistent, but individual characters themselves are usually not psychologically complex. The impossibility of answering questions about Barnaby's spiritual nature seems to reflect, not a complex but a fuzzy conception of character. And this fault in characterization weakens *Barnaby Rudge,* the power of which depends on unity of feeling and weaving moral strands into a unified theological fabric.

Dickens' defective characterization of Barnaby did not affect his depiction of Barnaby's parents, who were immediately recognizable as stock moral characters. Inviting readers to recall Gabriel Varden's warning not to trust to chance, Mary Rudge's experience taught that those who put their trust in God would eventually triumph over adversity. Quickly dismissing her, saying she crept through the novel "in a tediously lugubrious resignation," Edgar Johnson overlooked one of the book's most important sermons.[25] Believing in the efficacy of deathbed repentance, Dickens thought it was never too late for an individual—or, for that matter,

24. Cunningham, *A World without Souls,* p. 8. *Evangelical Magazine,* 2 (1794), 21.
25. Johnson, I, 330.

a society—to change its ways and be saved. While visiting him in prison, Mary Rudge begged her husband to confess his crimes and "implore the forgiveness of Heaven" (562–565). By making Mary Rudge the vehicle of this important doctrine, Dickens taught that all people, no matter how narrow their fields of benevolence, could contribute to the salvation of others and by implication to the stability of the country. Mary Rudge's struggle to do her Christian duty for humanity was recounted many times in religious journals. Of Silas Told, a sometime sailor and prison reformer in the eighteenth century, the *Arminian Magazine* wrote, for example, "This concludes the life of Mr. Silas Told, written by himself some time before his departure from this vale of tears, after having passed through a troublesome and laborious life with great fortitude and patience; being continually anxious for the good of his fellow-creatures, particularly the condemned malefactors in the several prisons in and about the metropolis; striving ardently, by all the means in his power, to promote their everlasting welfare: submitting meekly, for Christ's sake, to the ill treatment which he too often experienced, not only from prisoners and keepers, but from those, who ought rather to have encouraged and applauded him."[26]

From the same moral parentage, Mary Rudge passed through a laborious life with great fortitude and patience. Her Christian submission, visiting a condemned murderer in prison, and the ill treatment she received from him were all familiar features that enabled readers to recognize her

26. *Arminian Magazine*, 11 (1788), 406.

ancestry and the important note she added to the novel's moral orchestration.

Barnaby's father was an even more familiar character. Having broken the fundamental divine law like the Ancient Mariner, Rudge became an outcast from the human community. Conscience-ridden, he found no refuge from his crime. For Protestants, prayer and repentance provided the only refuge, and religious magazines were filled with accounts of criminals unable to bear the burden of their sins. Unlike those who confessed and were "created anew in Christ Jesus," Rudge hardened in sin. Despite his wife's pleadings, he refused to apply "to the throne of Grace for mercy" and consequently was damned.[27]

Rudge was not Dickens' only example of the corruption of a "stony heart." After the murder of his brother, Geoffrey Haredale became a recluse, implicitly denying both his responsibility for and the brotherhood of man. Toward the end of the novel, Haredale acknowledged his error, saying that his "spirit should have mixed with all God's great creation" (605). However like Rudge, Haredale's heart had hardened, and he found it impossible to embrace the spirit of Christianity or to forgive his brother's murderer and turn away Sir John's scorn with Gabriel Varden's strong mildness. "The great aversion," the *Methodist Magazine* wrote pointedly, "which we perceive in some persons to manifest a willingness to be speedily reconciled to one who has offended them, is almost sufficient to make us believe, that either, they have never read the Bible, or else, that they never resolved

27. *Methodist Magazine*, 21 (1798), 225. *Evangelical Magazine*, 2 (1794), 22.

to make the sacred precepts of that blessed Book the rule of their conduct." As a remedy for self-centered grief, Mrs. West preached the virtues of active benevolence. "Go, and relieve the wants of poverty, smooth the bed of sickness, alleviate the anguish of incurable grief, dissipate the gloom of ignorance," she urged her readers, "and if possible limit the ravages of vice." "Rise to the noble task for which you were called into existence. You cannot want employment," she stressed, "when you have to prepare yourself for eternity. You cannot be wretched while you can make your fellow-creatures happy." Like Mrs. Varden, however, Haredale did not rise to the noble task, and instead of assisting others in their journeys through "this troublesome world" and rejoicing in their successes, he turned selfishly inward, tormented by his "own sorrows." Moreover, this process was accelerated by the imperfections of Catholicism. Although scrupulously fair to Catholics during the riots, Dickens was not a friend to Catholicism. According to him Catholicism wrongly stressed dead ceremonies or the letter of Christianity instead of the vital spirit. Instead of promoting good works and the brotherhood of man, Catholic dogma divided the Christian community and impeded good deeds. In 1794 the *Evangelical Magazine* expressed an attitude to which Dickens would have subscribed. "Beads and pilgrimages, and relics, and all the retinue of *popish* ceremonies," the journal wrote, "are but substitutes for the love of God and our neighbour."[28]

28. *Evangelical Magazine*, 2 (1794), 22, 51. *Methodist Magazine*, 21 (1798), 151. West, *A Gossip's Story, and a Legendary Tale* (London, 1797), II, 134–135, and *The Sorrows of Selfishness; Or, the History Of Miss Richmore* (London, 1802), p. xvi.

Chapter 5

For the *Evangelical Magazine,* the sum of the divine law"
was love. In contrast, "the essence of depravity" consisted "in
the want of love to God and our neighbour; or in setting up
some other objects to the exclusion of them." Love created
harmony and ensured the stability of the state. With the marriages of Dolly and Joe and Emma and Edward, and with
red-faced children "staggering about the Maypole passage,"
the conclusion of *Barnaby Rudge* was almost a hymn to
Christian love. Christenings, birthdays, and wedding days
were celebrated at both the Maypole and the Golden Key.
Outside time, where Grip barely aged, this Maypole world
seemed another Eden. Hastily sketched, it appealed to
readers' imaginations as it glimmered coolly far from the
flames of the riots. The best of all worlds, a heaven on earth,
was within reach, Dickens implied, if Britons would embrace
the spirit of Christianity, by rejecting the Chesterfield code
and following "the moral instructions" taught in the pages
of *Barnaby Rudge.*[29]

29. *Evangelical Magazine,* 2 (1794), 96. *Arminian Magazine,* 10 (1787),
263.

Chapter 6
Dombey and Son and Unitarianism

Some fifty years ago in *The Dial,* George Santayana wrote: "It is remarkable, in spite of his ardent simplicity and openness of heart, how insensible Dickens was to the greater themes of the human imagination —religion, science, politics, art. He was a waif himself, and utterly disinherited. For example, the terrible heritage of contentious religions which fills the world seems not to exist for him. In this matter he was like a sensitive child, with a most religious disposition, but no religious ideas." When applied to *Barnaby Rudge* and *The Old Curiosity Shop,* Santayana's assessment is plainly wrong. In his later novels, however, Dickens often seems like a man with a religious disposition but with no religious doctrine. Evangelicalism reached its high-water mark in Dickens' novels in *Barnaby Rudge;* afterward Protestantism began to recede into the background of his fiction as his ambivalent attitude toward doctrine, marked by his inconsistent view of original sin, eventually hardened into a considered rejection of organized religion. To a large extent Dickens' theological progress mirrored the changing religious world of nineteenth-century Britain. According to Newman, evangelicalism was rapidly losing its momentum. After a great burst of emotional and creative energy early in the century, it had been found to have "no intellectual basis; no internal idea, no principle of unity, no theology." As a result, Newman wrote, evangelicals were "separating from each other" and the movement was melting away like a snow-drift."[1]

For Newman, there were but two choices left to the Christian pilgrim: "Catholic Truth and Rationalism." For Dickens, Catholicism with its seeming emphasis on doctrine and ceremony rather than good deeds was far beyond the moral pale. Moreover it was impossible for one who so emphasized childhood and humanizing fancy in his writings to become a dry-as-dust rationalist. Nevertheless, in melting away from evangelicalism, Dickens did drift toward rationalism, stopping near that eighteenth-century halfway house, latitudinarianism. In the world of Dickens' fiction *Dombey and Son* marked the twilight of systematic religion. In 1794 in a dialogue on doctrine, the *Evangelical Magazine* wrote, "Perhaps there is no one truth in the Scriptures of a more fundamental nature with respect to the gospel-way of salvation. I never knew a person verge towards the Arminian, the Arian, the Socinian, or the Antinomian schemes, without first entertaining diminutive notions of human depravity."[2] Although the *Magazine's* critical umbrella sheltered diverse heterodoxies, the principle was sound, especially in Dickens' case, where

1. George Santayana, "Dickens," in *The Dickens Critics*, ed. George Ford and Lauriate Lane, Jr. (Ithaca, 1961), pp. 136–137. John Henry Cardinal Newman, *Apologia Pro Vita Sua,* ed., Martin J. Svaglic (Oxford, 1967), p. 98.

2. *Evangelical Magazine*, 2 (1794), 96.

the path from original sin led to Socinianism or, as it was more popularly known, Unitarianism.

During his American trip in 1842, Dickens sought the acquaintance of William Ellery Channing, the prominent Boston Unitarian. In England two of Dickens' close friends were Unitarians: W. J. Fox and John Forster. After returning from America, Dickens himself attended the Essex Street Unitarian Chapel, and later took sittings in Edward Tagart's Unitarian chapel in Little Portland Street, becoming a lifelong friend of Tagart and a member of his congregation for two or three years. Resembling latitudinarianism, Unitarianism seemed particularly suited to Dickens' state of mind in the middle and late 1840's for he had grown progressively disillusioned with British political and theological establishments. In *Barnaby* he had bitterly criticized the ineffectual Lord Mayor and the time-serving members of Parliament.

Before journeying to the United States, Dickens had naively thought that American democracy offered an ideal governmental and social alternative to British oligarchy. But, as he said sadly, the America he saw was not the republic of his imagination. And when he returned from his travels, he seemed even more convinced that governmental establishments turned men into moral cripples. From politics it was but a short distance to religion, as the Established Church had long been considered a pillar of the Constitution. Similarly, when extended to the logical theological extreme, evangelicalism led to an Hebraic theocracy which rigorously cropped men's lives in hopes of turning them into "saints." "If sin be the cause of so large a portion of the miseries of human life," Hannah More asked in *Coelebs*, "must not that be the noblest charity which cures, or lessens, or prevents sin?" Looking hard at the abuses of doctrinaire Protestantism, not only with his head but with his heart, Dickens was rapidly becoming convinced that the prevention of sin could be, and quite often was, worse than the disease.[3]

In contrast, by denying or ignoring the doctrines of the Trinity, original sin, and the atonement while stressing New Testament ethics in general and the Sermon on the Mount in particular, Unitarianism seemed to offer the tolerant spirit of Christianity rather than the unbending letter. Moreover, Unitarianism's recent history of enduring and triumphing over suppression appealed to Dickens particularly at this time, when he was becoming convinced that governmental and ecclesiastical establishments were repressive. This I take to be part of the reason why he cultivated Sydney Smith, saying that of all the men he had heard of and had never met, he had the greatest curiosity to see and to know Smith. During the Napoleonic Wars, when Unitarians and broad church divines were rooted out of the Established Church, and in the case of the former, sometimes out of the country, Smith courageously fought for liberal policies in both church and state through the *Edinburgh Review*. Comparing him to Judas and saying that he was the greatest scoundrel ever to escape the gallows, outraged conservative periodicals accused him of being a Socinian and of dishonestly swearing assent to the Thirty-nine Articles. Although he denied the accusation, Smith's published sermons were so blatantly latitudinarian that the charge stuck, with the result that his ecclesiastical career was damaged. By the 1830's, however, the

3. Johnson, I, 378, 395–410, 464. More, *Coelebs*, II, 26–27.

political winds had shifted; and although the Whigs were too coldly pragmatic to appoint him to a bishopric, Smith was widely admired as the elder churchman of Whig ecclesiastical liberalism. After his death, the periodical press said that he had done more than any other divine in any age to shame bigotry, unmask hypocrisy, undermine abuses, and advance blessed reforms.[4]

It may go too far to say that in the middle and late 1840's Dickens envisioned himself as a latter-day Sydney Smith. But certainly during this period his religious views came to resemble those of Smith. Moreover, as he rejected abstract doctrine, he put more emphasis on personal benevolence, as Smith had repeatedly urged in the *Edinburgh Review*. For example, he made speeches for institutions like the Charitable Society for the Deaf and Dumb, and the Governesses' Benevolent Society, and supervised Miss Burdett Coutts's home for fallen women. In this decade Smith was such a powerful force in Dickens' mind that when his seventh son was born in April 1847, he named him after Smith.[5]

It should be stressed that although Dickens' view of evangelical doctrine both as repressive and as inhibiting practical benevolence was becoming widespread, it was not particularly accurate. The Sunday School movement and the *Cheap Repository* were lasting monuments to evangelical benevolence and provided the foundation upon which Dick-

4. House and Storey, *Letters* (1965), I, 546. For Unitarianism see Earl More Wilbur's splendid volumes, *A History of Unitarianism: Socinianism and Its Antecedents* and *A History of Unitarianism: In Transylvania, England, and America* (Cambridge, 1945, 1952). *Anti-Jacobin*, 29 (1808), 419–426. *Christian Examiner*, 86 (1869), 157.

5. Sydney Smith Haldimand Dickens died at sea as a young man.

ens rested the superstructures of his early novels. Typically, in *Some Thoughts for the New Year* the Claphams preached that a more heavenly earth was possible if Christians would accept responsibility for their fellows: "O, how many troubles and miseries there are in this land, which, if a few more of our independent ladies and gentlemen would be so good as to turn Christians, (I mean zealous Christians!), would presently be relieved"; "what a great number of poor cottagers are there who drag on life both in wickedness and misery for the want of being overlooked, and instructed and advised, and now and then assisted by their superiors who dwell near them? Here perhaps a whole parish is neglected through want of a christian parish officer; there the accounts of an hospital need examining, or a workhouse is given up to vice and ruin . . . Now these are the employments which constitute the calling of independent people. Christianity brings them to a strict sense of their responsibility . . . and at the same time enlarges their hearts in love to all their fellow creatures." This sort of moral urgency had long since penetrated Dickens' bloodstream and found the way to his heart. By the 1840's, however, he had become increasingly wary of the good intentions of "zealous Christians." And in his efforts to find a theological justification for his good deeds, he rejected evangelical Protestantism and embraced Unitarianism.[6]

The most striking evidence of his interest in Unitarianism is found in *The Life of Our Lord,* a child's life of Jesus based primarily on St. Luke and the Sermon on the Mount. Since the book was written for children, Phillip Collins has min-

6. *Some New Thoughts for the New Year,* Cheap Repository Tracts (London, 1796), pp. 16–17.

imized its importance. Although certainly intended for children, or at least the childlike adult with a religious disposition, the book was an accurate reflection, I think, of Dickens'
theological beliefs at the time. Resembling a Socinian tract,
it does not mention the orthodox doctrines of the Trinity,
original sin, and the atonement.[7] On the question of Christ's
divinity Dickens was markedly ambivalent. At the beginning
of the book he says that Jesus' father was Joseph, adding that
the angel telling the shepherds of his birth had said: "There
is a child born today in the City of Bethlehem near here, who
will grow up to be so good that God will love him as his own
son" (14). Later he wrote that on Jesus' baptism, God spoke
from the heavens saying: "This is my beloved Son, in whom
I am well pleased" (23–24).

Christ's divinity, however, was not crucial to the book's
didacticism, and Jesus appeared as a moral man asserting
universal brotherhood and the importance of active benevolence. Even the miracles that Dickens selected showed Jesus
performing good deeds: helping individuals by curing their
bodily ailments or forgiving their sins and relieving their
mental anxieties (30–52).

Focusing on this world, Unitarianism stressed the importance of good deeds. By ignoring doctrine, it avoided not only
the danger of Calvinistic misanthropy but also arguments
that strained to prove that the compulsion for benevolence
stemmed from an awareness of original sin. For Unitarians
the evil in the world was not in man but between men, and
the way to make men better was to improve their environ-

7. Dickens, *The Life of Our Lord* (London, 1934). Philip Collins,
Dickens and Education (London, 1963), pp. 54–60.

ments. Agreeing, Dickens preached to his children: "Never be proud or unkind, my dears, to any poor man, woman or child. If they are bad, think that they would have been better, if they had had kind friends, and good homes, and had been better taught. So, always try to make them better by kind persuading words; and always try to teach them and relieve them if you can" (28).

For Dickens, doctrine, no matter what the theology, now appeared to be the worm at the root of Jonah's gourd. In *The Life* he emphasized that the parable of the Good Samaritan illustrated brotherhood and the story of Dives and Lazarus taught that social barriers between people were unnatural and inhibited man's responsibility for man. Urging men to strip the inessentials from their faiths and adopt a truly Christian spirit, he combined Matthew 18:6 with Luke 9:48, making Jesus warn that "none but those who are as humble as little children shall enter into Heaven. Whosoever shall receive one such little child in my name receiveth me. But whosoever hurts one of them, it were better for him that he had a millstone tied about his neck, and were drowned in the depths of the sea. The angels are all children" (5). He concluded in a burst of moral fervor. "Remember!" he urged, "It is Christianity TO DO GOOD, always—even to those who do evil to us. It is Christianity to love our neighbour as ourself, and to do to all men as we would have them Do to us. It is christianity to be gentle, merciful, and forgiving, and to keep those qualities quiet in our own hearts, and never make a boast of them, or of our prayers or of our love of God, but always to shew that we love him by humbly trying to do right in everything" (124).

With Christ's divinity doubtful and Christianity shorn of doctrine, Dickens' faith resembled that of Santayana's simple child. Dickens, however, still believed that some sort of systematic Christianity, albeit nebulously latitudinarian, offered a panacea for the ills of society. Consequently, his next novel, *Dombey and Son*, became a parable-like corollary to *The Life of Our Lord*.

Dickens began Dombey just after finishing *The Life of Our Lord*. On June 28, 1846, he wrote John Forster, "Half of the children's New Testament to write, or pretty nearly. I set to work and did *that*. Next I cleared off the greater part of such correspondence as I had rashly pledged myself to; and then . . . BEGAN DOMBEY!" Departing from his usual method of composition, he planned much of the work before he began writing. So far as can be determined, his first six novels grew without a closely ordered plan, from week to week or month to month, depending on the type of parts-publication. The difference in organizing *Dombey* not only indicates a maturation of his narrative skills, but also implies that Dickens felt he had a message for society in mind before he began to preach.[8]

We should be careful, however, not to pin the message down too closely, for Dickens' best laid didactic intentions were always liable to go astray once he got deep into a novel. In March 1846 he told Forster that he intended to make pride the theme of *Dombey and Son*, much as he had made selfishness the theme of *Martin Chuzzlewit*. To contribute to this

8. John Forster, *The Life of Charles Dickens* (London, 1966), I, 395. Kathleen Tillotson and John Butt, *Dickens at Work* (London, 1957), pp. 90–96.

end, he helped design the cover that bound the issues for each month. On it pride was clearly emphasized. Approved in September 1846 before Dickens had written the book, the cover was, however, somewhat misleading. As Dickens got into the heart of the novel, his narrative and thematic plans shifted. Although a debate in Parliament was sketched in the upper right-hand corner of the cover, for example, no such scene is in the work. Similarly, although pride plays an important thematic role, it is not the dominant subject. Instead the novel mirrors Dickens' recent interest in Unitarianism, becoming, in fact, almost a Unitarian novel.[9]

Published with the last numbers of the novel in April 1848, the frontispiece provides more reliable evidence of Dickens' final thematic emphasis than either the monthly cover or his statement to Forster two years earlier. With angelic children kneeling at their feet and angels standing behind them, Paul and Florence Dombey are depicted seated in the center of the plate. In the clouds at the top of the plate are nineteen other angels busily playing harps, watching over Paul's sickbed, and waiting to crown him with a halo when he is carried into the heavens. From the one o'clock to the eleven o'clock positions on the plate, the narrative is sketched both allegorically and realistically. On the right-hand side, top to bottom, are depicted the death of Mrs. Dombey, with Doctor Parker Peps standing by holding his watch; Polly Toodle holding the baby Paul, while Florence and Miss Tox look on; Florence and Edith embracing; Carker craftily watching Edith while Major Bagstock, resembling an auctioneer, points at her with his cane; Dombey sitting straight-

9. Forster, II, 19.

backed while Edith flees and Florence cowers on the steps; and Mrs. Skewton being forced into the sea by an angel holding an empty hourglass and by a skeleton with a spear.

On the left, top to bottom, are scenes showing the death of little Paul, Paul being observed in school by Cornelia and Mr. Blimber, Paul sitting on the steps before Mr. Feeder and the clock, Paul sitting next to his father while a print with "cash" written on it hangs on the wall behind them, and Carker cringing in front of the train while a revenging angel shakes a lightening bolt at him. On the lower portion of the plate below the sketches of the narrative are emblematic sea scenes. In the novel the sea has a dual significance: it is one of the two primordial elements, the other being dust, from which all life comes and to which all life returns; and as a life and death force with which all the characters had come to terms, it represented eternity. In touch with vital Christianity the morally good characters understood it, were attracted by it, and were able to "sail" upon it.

In the frontispiece the sea is filled with creatures—cherubs in a boat, the wind with puffed cheeks, mermaids, Triton blowing on his horn, and Neptune or Proteus. At five o'clock on the plate, an angel in a sculling boat rows Miss Tox ashore, while next to her Major Bagstock is swept out to sea. Next to him a host of happy sea creatures protect Sol Gills. At eight o'clock, Walter crawls ashore amid the debris of the *Son and Heir*. On the beach he is shown greeting Florence, while Captain Cuttle dances gleefully. At nine o'clock, with her own child beside her, Florence helps her father ashore.

Actually something of a theological coda, the frontispiece helps to illustrate the extent to which Unitarianism pervaded

Dombey and Son. Although religious paraphernalia (angels, harps, haloes) cover the plate, significantly there are no overt Christian symbols such as the Cross. Moreover, the doctrines hinted at are at best latitudinarian and at worst heterodox. Ruling out a traditional hell, the plate shows those who were damned according to orthodox doctrine being swept out to sea—that is, degenerating into primitive elements. The plate did stress the efficacy of deathbed repentance. However, it is Florence rather than God who pulls Mr. Dombey out of the sea.

Once again Dickens had used children as lights to heaven. This time, however, his criticism of the tangible and intangible things of the world was stronger. "Cash" was practically meaningless in a perspective that included angels. Washing about in the sea, the goods of the *Son and Heir* were revealed to be trash, bearing little resemblance to those real riches upon which the Christian founded his eternal fortune. Among the things of the world, Dickens now emphasized fashionable education. In the plate Paul appears trapped in a prison cell, as the Blimbers hover over him forming two human, yet inhuman walls, while books and a globe press upon him as the other two.

Unitarianism had helped Dickens resolve his earlier uncertainty about original sin. Rejecting it out of hand, he now thought education was to blame for many of the evils he saw about him. Instead of teaching children to be better than the world, contemporary education, he seemed to think, built bad habits and so bent children that they conformed to the world. To escape the bondage of habit, or education, was difficult, if not impossible. In apologizing for never having concerned himself about their welfare, Mr. Morfin explained to Harriet and John Carker that "It's this same habit that confirms some of us who are capable of better things, in Lucifer's own pride and stubbornness—that confirms and deepens others of us in villainy—more of us in indifference—that hardens us from day to day, according to the temper of our clay, like images, and leaves us as susceptible to new impressions and convictions" (745).

At Mrs. Pipchin's and Blimber's Academy, fresh clay was baked in the kiln of fashionable education until it hardened into "young Chesterfields." At Charity Schools, under the patronage of the fashionable, poor children like Rob Toodle lost their capacity for better things. Tutored in the ways of the world by her mother, Edith hardened in pride and stubbornness until she was almost incapable of feeling. In contrast the "good" characters of *Dombey and Son*, Walter, Susan Nipper, and Florence did not receive fashionable educations and retained their moral spontaneity. In Mr. Toots's case, education happily did not take; and remaining innocently simple he was always benevolent and susceptible to new impressions and convictions.

Dombey was the novel's corrupted worldly man. First pictured jingling a gold watch chain which hung heavily below his coat, he was a prisoner of time and money. Because he was not a Christian, he did not understand the nature of eternity. Thinking that time passed slowly, he hurried Paul's studies, picking schools only on the basis of their cost. In contrast, the Christian Hero Captain Cuttle was unable to make money and was oblivious to time. Although his watch was broken, Captain Cuttle understood eternity and was superior to time, knowing how to control it if he had to, merely by setting his watch back half an hour in the morning and a quarter of an hour in the afternoon. Toying with the unpleasant connotation of "fashionable," Dickens called Sol Gills and Captain Cuttle "old fashioned." Indeed they were old fashioned, rejecting Dombey's chilling, modern ways and recognizing the ancient brotherhood of man. At the end of the novel, when Dombey's business has collapsed, Gills's investments have turned out successfully, and the world noted that Gills was ahead of his time. In truth, Solomon Gills was both ahead and behind the times, since his investments were eternal, not financial but spiritual.

Resembling the man of feeling in whom motions of compassion indicated virtue, Dickens' good characters wept freely. Only after Mr. Dombey wept was he able to ask Florence's forgiveness, and even then he had to become seriously ill and suffer for his sins before he could be reborn like a child, susceptible to new impressions and convictions. In contrast Mrs. Skewton had so hidden herself in "the Rock of Cosmetics," or, on another level, under the dogma of the world, that she became a grotesque female Chesterfield. Like Dombey she did not understand the nature of eternity; but instead of weeping her way out of time to forgiveness and paradise, she tried to make time stand still. Unlike Cuttle and Gills, who laid up spiritual treasures where moths and rust could not corrupt, she vainly treasured herself. Consequently at her death, like all the other vanities of this world, her dust returned to dust, and she ended like the goods of the *Son and Heir,* trash scattered at the edge of the sea.

Captain Cuttle is the book's ideal Christian. Every Sunday

night, Dickens wrote, he read the Sermon on the Mount and "although he was accustomed to quote the text, without book, after his own manner, he appeared to read it with as reverent an understanding of its heavenly spirit, as if he had got it all by heart in Greek, and had been able to write any number of fierce theological disquisitions on its every phrase" (543). In contrast, Rob Toodle, who had been subjected to the tutelage of the Charitable Grinders, stood bleakly as the product of contemporary religious education. Dickens used Rob Toodle to emphasize the difference between the vital spirit and the dead letter of religion. In her *Reflections,* Priscilla Wakefield had warned patrons of Charity Schools, like the one Rob attended, that "abstruse theological doctrines" were entirely unsuitable to the "great mass of the people" and "the custom of burthening their memories with verbal rituals" ought to be "carefully avoided, lest by disgusting them with the shadow, they should be alienated from the substance." All shadow, Rob's religious education never taught the substance of the Sermon on the Mount; and although he could rattle off the names of the tribes of Judah, he did not hesitate to become his brother's enemy and betray Captain Cuttle.[10]

Throughout *Dombey and Son,* Dickens illustrated the truth of the beatitudes. Blessed were those that mourned, the meek, the merciful, the pure in heart, and the peacemakers. Even the house—the dominant symbol of the book —was taken from the Sermon on the Mount: "Therefore," Jesus said, "whosoever heareth these sayings of mine, and doeth them, I will liken him unto a wise man, which built

10. Wakefield, p. 185.

his house upon a rock: And the rain descended, and the floods came, and the winds blew, and beat upon that house; and it fell not: for it was founded upon a rock. And every one that heareth these sayings of mine, and doeth them not, shall be likened unto a foolish man, which built his house upon the sand: And the rain descended, and the floods came, and the winds blew, and beat upon the house; and it fell: and great was the fall of it" (Matthew 7: 24–27).

For the wise reader, the novel itself was the "sayings"; the firm of Dombey and Son was the house built upon the sand; and the Wooden Midshipman was that founded upon a rock. Throughout the book, Dickens used houses almost like the degree marks on the *Evangelical Magazine's* Spiritual Barometer. Marking "the Progress of SIN and GRACE," the outward physical condition of a house revealed the inward spiritual condition of its owner. As Dombey was an almost spiritually dead prisoner of pride, so his house appeared as both a prison and a tomb. Standing black on the shady side of the street where the sun rarely shone, its barred cellar windows resembled cells. In the back yard two black, gaunt trees rattled like chains. After Mrs. Dombey's death, the oppressive atmosphere intensified. With the furniture shrouded like corpses, decay oozed throughout the house and "odours, as from vaults and damp places, came out of the chimneys" (21–22).

Closely reflecting Dombey's spiritual degeneration, the house deteriorated further after Paul's death. "Within doors," Dickens wrote, "curtains, drooping heavily lost their old folds and shapes, and hung like cumbrous palls. Hecatombs of furniture, still piled and covered up, shrunk like

imprisoned and forgotten men, and changed insensibly."
Keys rusted in the locks of doors while mildew and mould
began to lurk in closets and fungus trees grew in the corners
of the cellars. "Dust accumulated, nobody knew whence nor
how; spiders, moths, and grubs were heard of every day,"
and "rats began to squeak and scuffle in the night time,
through dark galleries they mined behind the panelling"
(319).

Before marrying Edith, Dombey redecorated the house.
But he was not able to stem the deterioration, for he had paid
attention to inessentials and his own conduct had not taken
"a heavenly direction." The rats were still behind the walls
of his clayey tenement, and the most expensive cosmetic
could not shore up his weakened spiritual beams. As false
curls, false eyebrows, false teeth, rouge, and gossamer para-
sols could not prevent Mrs. Skewton from turning to dust,
so frosted cupids could not bless Dombey's marriage with
love and happiness.

Like the education she provided, the soil around Mrs.
Pipchin's house was chalky, flinty, and sterile. Good Mrs.
Brown's house was a dustheap; and as she herself was but a
bit of rag and bone filled with the cinders of burned-out lust
and anger, so the dark room in which she put Florence was
piled with rags, bones, and cinders. In contrast stood the
Wooden Midshipman, with nothing of the tomb or prison
about it. Filled with old-fashioned instruments and lit by a
skylight, the shop, Dickens wrote, seemed "almost to become
a snug, sea-going, ship-shape concern, wanting only good
sea-room, in the event of an unexpected launch, to work its
way securely to any desert island in the world"(33).

As houses mirrored the spiritual condition of their owners, so churches, the house of God, reflected the spiritual condition of Britain. Having forsaken the spirit of the New Testament, the Established Church was moribund. With its tall shrouded pulpit, empty pews, grim organ, dusty matting, cold slabs, cadaverous light, and uncomfortable smell, the church at Paul's christening yawned like a grave (55–56). Later at Florence's wedding, the odor of decay seeped through the church. With an ancient dusty pew-opener, a dusty old beadle, and dusty ledges and cornices gray above the altar, the church seemed an aging house tottering upon sand (806–807).

Only the vital spirit of the Sermon on the Mount could breathe life back into the dry bones of Christianity. If this were not done, Dickens implied, not only individuals, but the nation itself would sicken and die like Mrs. Skewton. To impress the urgent need for spiritual reformation upon his readers, he intruded into the narrative and preached an 850-word jeremiad on the moral pestilence plaguing Britain. It had become natural, he wrote, "to be unnatural." Prisoners of a "single idea" or cooped "within a narrow range," men ignored their Christian responsibilities, with the result that "a long train of nameless sins against the natural affections and repulsions of mankind" had blighted "the innocent and spread the contagion among the pure." "Vainly attempt," he wrote metaphorically, "to think of any simple plant, or flower, or wholesome weed, that, set in this foetid bed, could have its natural growth, or put its little leaves off to the sun as GOD designed it" (646–648).

Although the sermon contained the seeds of Dickens' later

pessimistic novels, *Dombey and Son* was an ultimately optimistic book. And this, I think, was attributable to Dickens' interest in Unitarianism. Although Dombey's house fell, the Wooden Midshipman sailed on the sea of eternity. Although organized religion had hardened into but an image of the Christian spirit, Christianity was kept vitally alive in Florence and Captain Cuttle. Florence was able to save her father because Dickens believed that the ethics of the Sermon on the Mount provided a cure-all for the ills of society. Good triumphed over evil as Carker died and Rob the Grinder promised to reform. True to the spirit of the New Testament, Harriet Carker bathed Alice Marwood's cut foot. Later she saved Alice's soul; and as Alice died, she read her Christ's message of kindness and charity, "the blessed history, in which the blind lame palsied beggar, the criminal, the woman stained with shame, the shunned of all our dainty clay, has each a portion . . . [Harriet] read the ministry of Him who, through the round of human life, and all its hopes and griefs, from birth to death, from infancy to age, had sweet compassion for, and interest in, its every scene and stage, its every suffering and sorrow" (826–827).

Dombey and Son was at the theological fulcrum of Dickens' career as a writer. Having rejected Protestant doctrine, he still believed that "the blessed history" read by Alice Marwood could cure the pestilence threatening the country. By the time of *Bleak House* (1853), however, his attitude had changed. In *Practical Christianity*, Wilberforce had observed that it was difficult for a man to remain a Unitarian for a long time. Indeed more often than not, Wilberforce wrote, Unitarianism was but a "stage on the journey . . . from nominal orthodoxy to absolute infidelity."[11] Although he never "progressed" to infidelity, Unitarianism was, nevertheless, but a stage on Dickens' religious journey. By 1853 he had become convinced that although Sermon on the Mount offered individuals the best of all possible codes of personal conduct, it was an inadequate antidote for the evils pervading Britain. For Dickens there was no longer a simple solution to the problems of society, and the world of his novels grew darker. With fog smothering the countryside and Tulkinghorns, Smallweeds, and Vholeses growing about them, the Christian activists of *Bleak House* were less effective than their counterparts in *Dombey and Son*. Florence was transformed into Esther Summerson, no longer inviolable but disfigured by disease. Instead of raising a family and being at the center of an old-fashioned Christian order in London, Esther left the south of England for Yorkshire, metaphorically another country. The old-fashioned morality became truly old-fashioned, and Dickens' Christians, his Boffins and Boythorns, became eccentrics, out of place in the world and beleaguered by the forces of materialism and spiritual corruption.

11. Wilberforce, p. 475.

Afterword

"That light that shines upon some of us," Chadband said in *Bleak House*, was "the light of Terewth." A spiritual descendant of Boanerges Boiler, Chadband was one of the fortunate few blind enough to be able to see truth steadily and see it whole. For critics of literature, the light of truth is, alas, not so bright as it was for Dickens' evangelical divine. In *A Tale of the Times*, Mrs. West lamented that one of the misfortunes under which literature labored was that the title of a work no longer announced its intention. Books of travels, she noted, were often converted into "vehicles of politics" and "systems of legislation" while female letter-writers insinuated "the arcana of government" under the flowers of domestic pleasantry, and sometimes obliquely vindicated, or even recommended, "manners and actions at which female delicacy should blush, and female tenderness mourn." Although literary ladies seem to have become rather less delicate since Mrs. West's time, the difficulty of interpreting an author's intention has remained constant. If critics of today are not particularly disturbed when they find "descriptions which modesty cannot peruse" or "sophistical principles of false philosophy" lurking under the cover of a novel, they are, nevertheless, interested in the "light of Terewth" which shines up from a book's pages. Seeing that light as it really is has not been easy, however, since the Fall. In hopes of making that light which shines on me shine "upon some of us," I want to suggest several topics that could be examined with a view toward further determining the influence of evangelicalism and Sunday School education upon British fiction in the first half of the nineteenth century.

At a time when criticism seems tediously contrived, attempts should be made to rejuvenate a few critical bromides. To this end it might be fruitful to reexamine the marriages between sense and sensibility which are common in the nineteenth-century novel. Interesting studies could be made of popular religious novelists like John Cunningham, and comparisons made to the works of better known writers like Charlotte Brontë and Mrs. Gaskell. Perhaps the Silver Fork novels should be closely examined, to determine the extent to which such books were parodies of evangelical moral tales. Because Carlyle viewed novels as artful preparations of moral poison, he missed the rigorous morality beneath the frivolous façade of Bulwer's hilarious satire *Pelham* and condemned the book out of hand. Even the tossing eccentricity of Marryat's brilliant and widely satiric sea stories seems to rest upon a bedrock of Hebraic theology and to resemble the anecdotal sensationalism of the *Methodist* and *Evangelical Magazines*.

Evangelical theology strongly influenced early nineteenth-century literary and social criticism, most particularly that of Carlyle. For the source of his thought, we should look to his childhood education among the Burgher Seceders in Dumfriesshire and not to *Wilhelm Meister*. In that "peasant union" of nonconformist Protestants was cast the hard metal, in Emerson's words, of the age's "portable cathedral bell." Not just Carlyle's thought but also his literary style received its distinctive tone from his early evangelical experiences. His use of rhetorical repetition, biblical language, satire, metaphor, colloquialism, and moral characterization were literary techniques found on almost every page of evangelical journals. Moreover, staccato rhythms, striking expostulations, hyperbole, pithy sayings, comic interludes, and antithesis were the time-worn verbal tools of the field preacher. In 1794 the *Arminian Magazine* printed a letter from John Berridge to Charles Simeon, in which Berridge advised Simeon, who became the leading Anglican evangelical preacher, on the art of itinerant preaching. "When you open up your Commission," Berridge wrote, "begin with ripping up the Audience, and Moses will lend you a Carving Knife, which may often be whetted at his Grind-Stone. Lay open the universal sinfulness of nature, the darkness of the mind, the frowardness of the tempers,—the earthliness and sensuality of the affections:—Speak of the evil of sin in its Nature, its rebellion against God as our Benefactor, and contempt of his authority and Love;—Declare the evil of Sin in its effects, bringing all our sickness, pains, and sorrows, all the evils we feel, and all the evils we fear:—All innundations, fires, famines, pestilences, brawls, quarrels, fightings, Wars,—with Death, these present sorrows,—and Hell to receive all that die in sin." "When your Hearers have been well harrowed," Berridge advised, "and the clumps begin to fall, (which is seen by their hanging down the head), then bring out your CHRIST, and bring him out from the heart, thro' the lips, and tasting of his Grace while you publish it." "You must wave," Berridge concluded, "the Gospel Flag, and magnify the Saviour proudly; speak with a full mouth, that his Blood can wash away the foulest stains, and his grace subdue the stoutest corruptions."

Using a method similar to that of Berridge, Carlyle preached sermons on the state of Britain. Ripping up his readers, he laid bare the sins of the nation and predicted revolution in terms applicable to the Second Coming. Only by embracing the spirit of Christianity could the horrors of the Last Judgment be avoided. Repeatedly he harrowed his readers by exposing the darkness of the mind and the frowardness of the tempers. Then when he thought the clumps had begun to fall, he brought out his Christ. Although he did not wave a doctrinal Gospel Flag, for like Dickens, and indeed like most of his readers, he had drifted away from the letter of evangelicalism, Carlyle's traditional evangelical approach was partly responsible for his great success. Writing with a full mouth, he wove evangelical concerns that had long blown free in the air into a fabric that was at once strikingly familiar, and strikingly original because it was written rather than oral.

"What happens to the evangelical tradition in literature after the 1850's" ought to be the amber that imprisons many critical gadflies. Perhaps one should begin with Mrs. Gaskell's Unitarianism and her appeal to Dickens. Trollope with his criticism of abstractions and celebration of good deeds is also important. Crossing the ocean with Thomas Hughes, evangelicalism dominated novels written for juveniles in the United States in the last half of the nineteenth century. Particularly interesting are the books of William T. Adams, more familiarly known to his boy readers as Oliver Optic. Even for those modern novels that are not particularly evangelical or particularly moral, the conventions and metaphors of the evangelical tradition provide an instructive range of critical reference. At the end of Dreiser's *Sister Carrie*, twentieth-century fiction's Little Nell sits in her rocking chair, a pilgrim always moving but going nowhere. Black humor and existential despair often seem to reflect the anxieties of writers who as they walk through "the wilderness of this world" light "on a certain place," where is "a Denn" but who are unable to dream "a Dream."

Not to belabor a point, it may be that the greatness of the nineteenth-century novel depends upon the moral tradition of British fiction. For my part, I think that nineteenth-century writers' quarrels with or embodiments of evangelicalism gave the Victorian novel a philosophic and emotional unity that seems conspicuously absent in much contemporary fiction. Macaulay called *Coelebs* "a framework for better things." Perhaps that is what a great novel must be.

Index

Index

Index

Gospel Magazine, The, 136–37, 139; quotation from, 136–37
Graveyard, as instructional aid, 119–21
Graveyard School of poetry, 119 n.
Green, John Richard, *History of the English People,* 11
Guardian of Education, 30; quotations from, 48, 54–55, 66, 83

Hazlitt, William, 30
Hill, Aaron, 5
Hill, Rowland, *Village Dialogues,* 62, 129–30
Historical novel, more respectable than fiction, 96
Holland, Henry Richard, Lord, 37
Horne, George, 18
Horne, William Andrew (subject of biography), 67–69
Hoxton Academy (Sunday School), 32
Hughes, Thomas, 172

Jacobinism, Jacobins, 38, 40, 41
Johnson, Edgar, *Charles Dickens,* 108, 109 n., 123
Johnson, Samuel, 7, 100–1
Jones, William, *Jubilee Memorial,* 56

Kay-Stuttleworth, active in Sunday School movement, 12
Kilner, Dorothy, 28
Kilner, Mary Ann, *The Adventures of a Pincushion,* 29
Kilpin, the Reverend Samuel, 61
Kirby, Joshua, 20

Lamb, Charles, 29
Lamb, Mary, 29
Latitudinarians, 4–5, 10, 22, 39, 126, 150
Leadbeater, Mary, *Cottage Dialogues among the Irish Peasantry,* 62, 84, 85
Lefevre, Charles (character), v, vi
Lever, Charles, 60
Locke, John, *Essay Concerning Human Understanding,* 58
London Magazine, 7
London Review, quotations from, 93, 94
Louis XVI, 37

179

Index